CAMBRIDGE LIBRARY COLLECTION

Books of enduring scholarly value

Medieval History

This series includes pioneering editions of medieval historical accounts by eye-witnesses and contemporaries, collections of source materials such as charters and letters, and works that applied new historiographical methods to the interpretation of the European middle ages. The nineteenth century saw an upsurge of interest in medieval manuscripts, texts and artefacts, and the enthusiastic efforts of scholars and antiquaries made a large body of material available in print for the first time. Although many of the analyses have been superseded, they provide fascinating evidence of the academic practices of their time, while a considerable number of texts have still not been re-edited and are still widely consulted.

The Forme of Cury, a Roll of Ancient English Cookery

One of the oldest surviving English-language cookbooks, this fascinating work was originally compiled in the late fourteenth century by the master cooks at the court of Richard II. It contains nearly 200 recipes for the preparation of everyday dishes as well as elaborate banquets. Here we find roasts, stews, jellies and custards alongside dishes that call for highly prized spices or animals such as curlews and porpoises. This 1780 transcription, from the manuscript then belonging to Gustavus Brander and now in the British Library, was made by the Anglican clergyman and antiquary Samuel Pegge (1704–96). Ordained in 1730 and elected a fellow of the Society of Antiquaries in 1751, Pegge briefly discusses in his preface the history of cooking since antiquity, while his annotations to the text elucidate the medieval vocabulary. Among related items forming an intriguing appendix are rolls of provisions from the time of Henry VIII.

T0370808

Cambridge University Press has long been a pioneer in the reissuing of out-of-print titles from its own backlist, producing digital reprints of books that are still sought after by scholars and students but could not be reprinted economically using traditional technology. The Cambridge Library Collection extends this activity to a wider range of books which are still of importance to researchers and professionals, either for the source material they contain, or as landmarks in the history of their academic discipline.

Drawing from the world-renowned collections in the Cambridge University Library and other partner libraries, and guided by the advice of experts in each subject area, Cambridge University Press is using state-of-the-art scanning machines in its own Printing House to capture the content of each book selected for inclusion. The files are processed to give a consistently clear, crisp image, and the books finished to the high quality standard for which the Press is recognised around the world. The latest print-on-demand technology ensures that the books will remain available indefinitely, and that orders for single or multiple copies can quickly be supplied.

The Cambridge Library Collection brings back to life books of enduring scholarly value (including out-of-copyright works originally issued by other publishers) across a wide range of disciplines in the humanities and social sciences and in science and technology.

The Forme of Cury, a Roll of Ancient English Cookery

Compiled, about A.D. 1390,
by the Master-Cooks of King Richard II

EDITED BY SAMUEL PEGGE

CAMBRIDGE
UNIVERSITY PRESS

CAMBRIDGE
UNIVERSITY PRESS

University Printing House, Cambridge, CB2 8BS, United Kingdom

Cambridge University Press is part of the University of Cambridge.
It furthers the University's mission by disseminating knowledge in the pursuit of
education, learning and research at the highest international levels of excellence.

www.cambridge.org
Information on this title: www.cambridge.org/9781108076203

© in this compilation Cambridge University Press 2015

This edition first published 1780
This digitally printed version 2015

ISBN 978-1-108-07620-3 Paperback

This book reproduces the text of the original edition. The content and language reflect
the beliefs, practices and terminology of their time, and have not been updated.

Cambridge University Press wishes to make clear that the book, unless originally published
by Cambridge, is not being republished by, in association or collaboration with,
or with the endorsement or approval of, the original publisher or its successors in title.

Samuel Pegge A.M. S.A.S.

A.D. MDCCLXXXV. Æt. 81.

Impensis et ex voto **Gustav Brander** *Armr.*

SIBI ET AMICIS.

THE
FORME OF CURY,
A ROLL
OF
ANCIENT ENGLISH COOKERY,

Compiled, about A. D. 1390, by the
Mafter-Cooks of King RICHARD II,

Prefented afterwards to Queen ELIZABETH,
by EDWARD Lord STAFFORD,

And now in the Poffeffion of GUSTAVUS BRANDER, Efq.

Illuftrated with N O T E S,

And a copious I N D E X, or G L O S S A R Y.

A M A N U S C R I P T of the E D I T O R, of the
fame Age and Subject, with other congruous
Matters, are fubjoined.

" —— ingeniofa gula eft."   MARTIAL.

L O N D O N,
PRINTED BY J. NICHOLS.
PRINTER TO THE SOCIETY OF ANTIQUARIES.
M DCC LXXX.

T O

GUSTAVUS BRANDER, Efq.
F.R.S. F.S.A. and Cur. Brit. Muf.

S I R,

I RETURN your very curious Roll of Cookery, and I truft with fome Intereft, not full I confefs nor legal, but the utmoft which your Debtor, from the fcantinefs of his ability, can at prefent afford. Indeed, confidering your refpectable fituation in life, and that diffufive fphere of knowledge and fcience in which you are acting, it muft be exceedingly difficult for any one, how well furnifhed foever, completely to anfwer your juft, or

even

even moſt moderate demands. I intreat the favour of you, however, to accept for once this ſhort payment in lieu of better, or at leaſt as a public teſtimony of that profound regard wherewith I am,

S I R,

Your affectionate friend,

and moſt obliged ſervant,

St. George's day,
1780.   S. P E G G E.

P R E-

P R E F A C E

TO THE

CURIOUS ANTIQUARIAN READER.

WITHOUT beginning *ab ovo* on a fubject fo light (a matter of importance, however, to many a modern Catius or Amafinius), by inveftigating the origin of the Art of Cookery, and the nature of it as practifed by the Antediluvians [a]; without dilating on the feveral particulars concerning it afterwards

---

[a] If, according to Petavius and Le Clerc, the world was created in autumn, when the fruits of the earth were both plentiful and in the higheft perfection, the firft man had little occafion for much culinary knowledge: roafting or boiling the cruder productions, with modes of preferving thofe which were better ripened, feem to be all that was neceffary for him in the way of *Cury*. And even after he was difplaced from Paradife, I conceive, as many others do, he was not permitted the ufe of animal food [Gen. i. 29.]; but that this was indulged to us, by an enlargement of our charter, after the Flood, Gen. ix. 3. But, without wading any further in the argument here, the reader is referred to Gen. ii. 8. feq. iii. 17. feq. 23.

b   amongft

amongſt the Patriarchs, as found in the Bible [b], I ſhall turn myſelf immediately, and without further preamble, to a few curſory obſervations reſpecting the Greeks, Romans, Britons, and thoſe other nations, Saxons, Danes, and Normans, with whom the people of this nation are more cloſely connected.

The Greeks probably derived ſomething of their ſkill from the Eaſt, (from the Lydians principally, whoſe cooks are much celebrated, [c]) and ſomething from Egypt. A few hints concerning Cookery may be collected from Homer, Ariſtophanes, Ariſtotle, &c. but afterwards they poſſeſſed many authors on the ſubject, as may be ſeen in Athenæus [d]. And as Diætetics were eſteemed a branch of the ſtudy of medicine, as alſo they were afterwards [e], ſo many of thoſe authors were Phyſicians; and *the Cook* was undoubtedly a character of high reputation at Athens [f].

---

[b] Geneſis xviii. xxvii. Though their beſt repaſts, from the politeneſs of the times, were called by the ſimple names of *Bread*, or a *Morſel of bread*, yet they were not unacquainted with modes of dreſſing fleſh, boiling, roaſting, baking; nor with ſauce, or ſeaſoning, as ſalt and oil, and perhaps ſome aromatic herbs. Calmet v. Meats and Eating. and qu. of honey and cream. ibid.

[c] Athenæus, lib. xii. cap. 3.

[d] Athenæus, lib. xii. cap. 3. et Caſaubon. See alſo Liſter ad Apicium, præf. p. ix. Jungerm. ad Jul. Pollucem, lib. vi. c. 10.

[e] See below. ' Tamen uterque [Torinus et Humelbergius] hæc ſcripta [i. e. Apicii] ad medicinam vendicarunt.' Liſter, præf. p. iv. viii. ix.

[f] Athenæus, p. 519. 660.

As

As to the Romans; they would of courſe borrow much of their culinary arts from the Greeks, though the Cook with them, we are told, was one of the loweſt of their ſlaves [g]. In the latter times, however, they had many authors on the ſubject as well as the Greeks, and the practitioners were men of ſome ſcience [h], but, unhappily for us, their compoſitions are all loſt except that which goes under the name of Apicius; concerning which work and its author, the prevailing opinion now ſeems to be, that it was written about the time of *Heliogabalus* [i], by one *Cælius*, (whether *Aurelianus* is not ſo certain) and that *Apicius* is only the title of it [k]. However, the compilation, though not in any great repute, has been ſeveral times publiſhed by learned men.

The Aborigines of Britain, to come nearer home, could have no great expertneſs in Cookery, as they had no oil, and we hear nothing of their butter. They uſed only ſheep and oxen, eating neither hares, though ſo greatly eſteemed at Rome, nor hens, nor geeſe, from a notion of ſuperſtition. Nor did they eat fiſh. There was little corn in the interior part of the

---

[g] Priv. Life of the Romans, p. 171. Liſter's Præf. p. iii. but ſee Ter. An. i. 1. Caſaub. ad Jul. Capitolin. cap. 5.

[h] Caſaub. ad Capitolin. l. c.

[i] Liſter's Præf. p. ii. vi. xii.

[k] Fabric. Bibl. Lat. tom. II. p. 794. Hence Dr. Bentley ad Hor. ii. ſerm. 8. 29. ſtiles it *Pſeudapicius*. Vide Liſterum, p. iv.

iſland,

ifland, but they lived on milk and flefh[1]; though it is exprefsly afferted by Strabo that they had no cheefe[m]. The later Britons, however, well knew how to make the beft ufe of the cow, fince, as appears from the laws of *Hoel Dda*, A. D. 943, this animal was a creature fo effential, fo common and ufeful in Wales, as to be the ftandard in rating fines, &c.[n].

Hengift, leader of the Saxons, made grand entertainments for king Vortigern[o], but no particulars have come down to us; and certainly little exquifite can be expected from a people then fo extremely barbarous as not to be able either to read or write. ' Barbari homines a feptentrione, (they are the words ' of Dr. Lifter) cafeo et ferina fubcruda victitantes, ' omnia condimenta adjectiva refpuerunt'[p].

Some have fancied, that as the Danes imported the cuftom of hard and deep drinking, fo they likewife introduced the practice of gormandizing, and that this word itfelf is derived from *Gormund*, the name of that Danifh king whom Ælfred the Great per-

[1] Cæfar de B. G. v. § 10,

[m] Strabo, lib. iv. p. 290. Pegge's Effay on Coins of Cunob. p. 95.

[n] Archæologia, iv. p. 61. Godwin, de Præful. p. 596. feq.

[o] Malmfb. p. 9, Galfr. Mon. vi. 12.

[p] Lifter. ad Apic. p. xi. where fee more to the fame purpofe,

fuaded

fuaded to be chriftened, and called Æthelftane q.
Now 'tis certain that Hardicnut ftands on record as
an egregious glutton r, but he is not particularly fa-
mous for being a *curious Viander*; 'tis true again, that
the Danes in general indulged exceffively in feafts
and entertainments s, but we have no reafon to ima-
gine any elegance of Cookery to have flourifhed
amongft them. And though Guthrum, the Danifh
prince, is in fome authors named *Gormundus* t; yet
this is not the right etymology of our Englifh word
Gormandize, fince it is rather the French *Gourmand*,
or the Britifh *Gormod* u. So that we have little to fay
as to the Danes.

I fhall take the later Englifh and the Normans together, on account of the intermixture of the two
nations after the Conqueft, fince, as lord Lyttelton
obferves, the Englifh accommodated themfelves to the
Norman manners, except in point of temperance in
eating and drinking, and communicated to them their
own habits of drunkennefs and immoderate feafting x.
Erafmus alfo remarks, that the Englifh in his time

q Spelm. Life of Ælfred, p. 66, Drake, Eboracum. Append.
p. civ.

r Speed's Hiftory.

s Monf. Mallet, cap. 12.

t Wilkins, Concil. I. p. 204. Drake, Ebor. p. 316. Append.
p. civ. cv.

u Menage, Orig. v. Gourmand.

x Lord Lyttelton, Hift. of H. II. vol. iii. p. 49.

were

were attached to *plentiful and splendid tables*; and the same is observed by Harrison [y]. As to the Normans, both William I. and Rufus made grand entertainments [z]; the former was remarkable for an immense paunch, and withal was so exact, so nice and curious in his repasts [a], that when his prime favourite William Fitz-Osberne, who as steward of the household had the charge of the Cury, served him with the flesh of a crane scarcely half-roasted, he was so highly exasperated, that he lifted up his fist, and would have strucken him, had not Eudo, appointed *Dapifer* immediately after, warded off the blow [b].

Dapifer, by which is usually understood *steward of the king's household* [c], was a high officer amongst the Normans; and *Larderarius* was another, clergymen

[y] Harrison, Descript. of Britain, p. 165, 166.

[z] Stow, p. 102. 128.

[a] Lord Lyuelton observes, that the Normans were delicate in their food, but without excess. Life of Hen. II. vol. III. p. 47.

[b] Dugd. Bar. I. p. 109. Henry II. served to his son. Lord Lyttelton, IV. p. 298.

[c] Godwin de Praesul. p. 695, renders *Carver* by *Dapifer*, but this I cannot approve. See Thoroton. p. 23. 28. Dugd. Bar. I. p. 441. 620. 109. Lib. Nig. p. 342. Kennet, Par. Ant. p. 119. And, to name no more, Spelm. in voce. The *Carver* was an officer inferior to the *Dapifer*, or *Steward*, and even under his control. Vide Lel. Collect. VI. p. 2. And yet I find Sir Walter Manny when young was carver to Philippa queen of king Edward III. Barnes Hist. of E. III. p. 111. The *Steward* had the name of *Dapifer*, I apprehend, from serving up the first dish. V. supra.

then

then often occupying this poſt, and ſometimes made biſhops from it [d]. He was under the *Dapifer*, as was likewiſe the *Cocus Dominicæ Coquinæ*, concerning whom, his aſſiſtants and allowances, the *Liber Niger* may be conſulted [e]. It appears further from *Fleta*, that the chief cooks were often providers, as well as dreſſers, of victuals [f]. But *Magiſter Coquinæ*, who was an eſquire by office, ſeems to have had the care of pourveyance, A. D. 1340 [g], and to have nearly correſponded with our *clerk of the kitchen*, having authority over the cooks [h]. However, the *Magnus Coquus, Coquorum Præpoſitus, Coquus Regius,* and *Grans Queux,* were officers of conſiderable dignity in the palaces of princes; and the officers under them, according to Du Freſne, were in the French court A. D. 1385, much about the time that our Roll was made, ' Queus, Aideurs, Aſteurs, Paiges, Souffleurs, ' Enfans, Sauſſiers de Commun, Sauſſiers devers le ' Roy, Sommiers, Poulliers, Huiſſiers' [i].

In regard to religious houſes, the Cooks of the greater foundations were officers of conſequence,

[d] Sim. Dunelm. col. 227. Hoveden, p. 469. Malmſ. de Pont. p. 286.

[e] Lib. Nig. Scaccarii, p. 347.

[f] Fleta, II. cap. 75.

[g] Du Freſne, v. Magiſter.

[h] Du Freſne, ibid.

[i] Du Freſne, v. Coquus. The curious may compare this Liſt with Lib. Nig. p 347.

though

though under the Cellarer ^k, and if he were not a monk, he neverthelefs was to enjoy the portion of a monk ^l. But it appears from Somner, that at Chrift Church, Canterbury, the *Lardyrer* was the firft or chief cook ^m; and this officer, as we have feen, was often an ecclefiaftic. However, the great Houfes had Cooks of different ranks ⁿ; and manors and churches^o were often given *ad cibum* and *ad victum monachorum* ^p. A fifhing at Lambeth was allotted to that purpofe ^q. But whether the Cooks were Monks or not, the *Magiftri Coquinæ*, Kitcheners, of the monafteries, we may depend upon it, were always monks; and I think they were moftly ecclefiaftics elfewhere: thus when Cardinal Otto, the Pope's legate, was at Oxford, A. 1238, and that memorable fray happened between his retinue and the ftudents, the *Magifter Coquorum* was the Legate's brother, and was there

---

^k In Somner, Ant. Cant. Append. p. 36. they are under the *Magifter Coquinæ*, whofe office it was to purvey; and there again the chief cooks are proveditors; different ufages might prevail at different times and places. But what is remarkable, the *Coquinarius*, or Kitchener, which feems to anfwer to *Magifter Coquinæ*, is placed before the Cellarer in Tanner's Notitia, p. xxx. but this may be accidental.

^l Du Frefne, v. Coquus.

^m Somner, Append. p. 36

ⁿ Somner, Ant. Cant. Append. p. 36.

^o Somner, p. 41.

^p Somner, p. 36, 37. 39, fæpius.

^q Somner, l. c.

killed.

killed [r]. The reason given in the author, why a person so nearly allied to the Great Man was assigned to the office, is this, ' Ne procuraretur aliquid vene- ' norum, quod nimis [i. e. valde] timebat legatus;' and it is certain that poisoning was but too much in vogue in these times, both amongst the Italians and the good people of this island [s]; so that this was a post of signal trust and confidence. And indeed after- wards, a person was employed to *taste*, or *take the assaie*, as it was called [t], both of the messes and the water in the ewer [u], at great tables; but it may be doubted whether a particular person was appointed to this service, or it was a branch of the *Sewer's* and cup-bearer's duty, for I observe, the *Sewer* is sometimes called *Præguflator* [x], and the cup-bearer tastes the water elsewhere [y]. The religious houses, and their presidents, the abbots and priors, had their days of *Gala*, as likewise their halls for strangers, whom, when persons of rank, they often entertained with splendour and magnificence. And as for the secular clergy, archbishops and bishops, their feasts,

[r] M. Paris, p4. 69.

[s] Dugd. Bar. I. p. 45. Stow, p. 184. M. Paris, p. 377. 517. M. Weftm. p. 364.

[t] Lel. Collectan. VI. p. 7. feq.

[u] Ibid. p. 9. 13.

[x] Compare Leland, p. 3. with Godwin de Præful. p. 695. and fo Junius in Etymol. v. Sewer.

[y] Leland, p. 8, 9. There are now *two yeomen of the mouth* in the king's household.

c

of which we have fome upon record [z], were fo fuperb, that they might vie either with the regal entertainments, or the pontifical fuppers of ancient
Rome (which became even proverbial [a]), and certainly could not be dreffed and fet out without a large
number of Cooks [b]. In fhort, the fatirifts of the
times before, and about the time of, the Reforma-
tion, are continually inveighing againft the high-
living of the bifhops and clergy; indeed luxury was
then carried to fuch an extravagant pitch amongft
them, that archbifhop Cranmer, A. 1541, found it
neceffary to bring the fecular clergy under fome rea-
fonable regulation in regard to the furnifhing of their
tables, not excepting even his own [c].

After this hiftorical deduction of the *Ars coquina-
ria*, which I have endeavoured to make as fhort as
poffible, it is time to fay fomething of the Roll which

[z] That of George Neville, archbifhop of York, 6 Edw. IV. and
that of William Warham, archbifhop of Canterbury, A. D. 1504.
Thefe were both of them inthronization-feafts. Leland, Collectan.
VI. p. 2 and 16 of Appendix. They were wont *minuere fangui-
nem* after thefe fuperb entertainments, p. 32.

[a] Hor. II. Od. xiv. 28. where fee Monf. Dacier.

[b] Sixty-two were employed by archbifhop Neville. And the hire
of cooks at archbifhop Warham's feaft came to 23 l. 6 s. 8 d.

[c] Strype, Life of Cranmer, p. 451, or Lel. Coll. ut fupra, p. 38.
Sumptuary laws in regard to eating were not unknown in ancient
Rome. Erafm. Colloq. p. 81. ed. Schrev. nor here formerly, fee
Lel. Coll. VI. p. 36. for 5 Ed. II.

is

is here given to the public, and the methods which the Editor has purſued in bringing it to light.

This vellum Roll contains 196 *formulæ,* or recipes, and belonged once to the earl of Oxford [d]. The late James Weſt eſquire bought it at the Earl's ſale, when a part of his MSS were diſpoſed of; and on the death of the gentleman laſt mentioned it came into the hands · of my highly-eſteemed friend, the preſent liberal and moſt communicative poſſeſſor. It is preſumed to be one of the moſt ancient remains of the kind now in being, riſing as high as the reign of king Richard II. [e]. However, it is far the largeſt and moſt copious collection of any we have; I ſpeak as to thoſe times. To eſtabliſh its authenticity, and even to ſtamp an additional value upon it, it is the identical Roll which was preſented to queen Elizabeth, in the 28th year of her reign, by lord Stafford's heir, as appears from the following addreſs, or inſcription, at the end of it, in his own hand-writing : ' Antiquum hoc monumentum oblatum et miſ ' ſum eſt majeſtati veſtræ viceſimo ſeptimo die menſis ' Julij, anno regni veſtri fæliciſſimi viceſimo viij ab

---

[d] I preſume it may be the ſame Roll which Mr. Hearne mentions in his Lib. Nig. Scaccarii, I. p. 346. See alſo three different letters of his to the earl of Oxford, in the Brit. Muſ. in the ſecond of which he ſtiles the Roll *a piece of antiquity, and a very great rarity indeed.* Harl. MSS. N° 7523.

[e] See the Proem.

' humi-

' humilimo veftro fubdito, veftræq majeftati fideliffimo
‘ E. Stafford,
‘ Hæres domus fubverfæ Buckinghamienf.’ [f]

The general obfervations I have to make upon it
are thefe : many articles, it feems, were in vogue in
the fourteenth century, which are now in a manner
obfolete, as cranes, curlews, herons, feals [g], por-
poifes, &c. and, on the contrary, we feed on fundry fowls which are not named either in the Roll, or
the Editor's MS. [h] as quails, rails, teal, woodcocks,
fnipes, &c. which can fcarcely be numbered among
the *fmall birds* mentioned 19. 62. 154. [i]. So as to
fifh, many fpecies appear at our tables which are not
found in the Roll, trouts, flounders, herrings, &c. [k].
It were eafy and obvious to dilate here on the variations of tafte at different periods of time, and the
reader would probably not diflike it ; but fo many
other particulars demand our attention, that I fhall
content myfelf with obferving in general, that where-

[f] This lord was grandfon of Edward duke of Bucks, beheaded
A. 1521, whofe fon Henry was reftored in blood ; and this Edward,
the grandfon, born about 1571, might be 14 or 15 years old when
he prefented the Roll to the Queen.

[g] Mr. Topham's MS. has *focas* among the fifh ; and fee archbifhop Nevil's Feaft, 6 E. IV. to be mentioned below.

[h] Of which fee an account below.

[i] See Northumb. Book, p. 107, and Notes.

[k] As to carps, they were unknown in England t. R. II. Fuller,
Worth. in Suffex, p. 98. 113. Stow, Hift. 1038.

as a very able *Italian* critic, *Latinus Latinius*, paſſed a ſiniſter and unfavourable cenſure on certain ſeemingly ſtrange medlies, difguſting and prepoſterous meſſes, which we meet with in *Apicius*; Dr. *Liſter* very ſenſibly replies to his ſtriċtures on that head, ' That theſe meſſes are not immediately to be rejeċted, ' becauſe they may be diſpleaſing to ſome. *Plutarch* ' teſtifies, that the ancients diſliked *pepper* and the ' four juice of lemons, infomuch that for a long time ' they only uſed theſe in their wardrobes for the fake ' of their agreeable ſcent, and yet they are the moſt ' wholeſome of all fruits. The natives of the *Weſt* ' *Indies* were no leſs averſe to *falt*; and who would ' believe that *hops* ſhould ever have a place in our ' common beyerage [1], and that we ſhould ever think ' of qualifying the ſweetneſs of malt, through good ' houſewifry, by mixing with it a fubſtance ſo egre- ' giouſly bitter? Moſt of the *American* fruits are ex- ' ceedingly odoriferous, and therefore are very dif- ' guſting at firſt to us *Europeans*: on the contrary, our ' fruits appear inſipid to them, for want of odour. ' There are a thouſand inſtances of things, would ' we recolleċt them all, which though diſagreeable to ' taſte are commonly aſſumed into our viands; indeed, ' *cuſtom* alone reconciles and adopts fauces which are ' even nauſeous to the palate. *Latinus Latinius* there-

---

[1] The Italians ſtill call the hop *cattiva erba*. There was a petition againſt them t. H. VI. Fuller, Worth. p. 317; &c. Evelyn, Sylva, p. 201. 469. ed. Hunter.

' fore

' fore very rashly and absurdly blames *Apicius*, on
' account of certain preparations which to him, for-
' sooth, were disrelishing [m]. In short it is a known
maxim, that *de gustibus non est disputandum*;

And so Horace to the same purpose :

' Tres mihi convivæ prope dissentire videntur,
' Poscentes vario multum diversa palato.
' Quid dem? quid non dem? renuis tu quod jubet
  ' alter.
' Quod petis, id sane est invisum acidumque
  ' duobus.

Hor. II. Epist. ii.

And our Roll sufficiently verifies the old observation
of Martial — *ingeniosa gula est*,

Our Cooks again had great regard to the eye, as
well as the taste, in their compositions; *flourishing*
and *strewing* are not only common, but even leaves of
trees gilded, or silvered, are used for ornamenting
messes, see N° 175 [n]. As to colours, which perhaps
would chiefly take place in suttleties, blood boiled
and fried (which seems to be something singular)
was used for dying black, 13. 141. saffron for yel-

---

[m] Lister, Præf. ad Apicium, p. xi.

[n] So we have *lozengs of goldc*. Lcl. Colle&. IV. p. 227. and a
wild boar's head *gylt*, p. 294, A peacock with *gylt ncb*. VI. p. 6,
Leche Lambart gylt, ibid.

low,

low, and ſanders for red[o]. Alkenet is alſo uſed for colouring[p], and mulberries[q]; amydon makes white, 68; and turneſole[r] *pownas* there, but what this colour is the Editor profeſſes not to know, unleſs it be intended for another kind of yellow, and we ſhould read *jownas*, for *jaulnas*, orange-tawney. It was for the purpoſe of gratifying the ſight that *ſotiltees* were introduced at the more ſolemn feaſts. Rabelais has comfits of an hundred colours.

Cury, as was remarked above, was ever reckoned a branch of the Art Medical; and here I add, that the verb *curare* ſignifies equally to dreſs victuals[s], as to cure a diſtemper; that every body has heard of *Doctor Diet*, *kitchen phyſick*, &c. while a numerous band of medical authors have written *de cibis et alimentis*, and have always claſſed diet among the *non-naturals*; ſo they call them, but with what propriety they beſt know. Hence Junius ‘ Δίαιτα Græcis eſt ‘ victus, ac ſpeciatim certa victûs ratio, qualis a *Me-* ‘ *dicis* ad tuendam valetudinem præſcribitur[t].’ Our

[o] N° 68. 20. 58. See my friend Dr. Percy on the Northumberland-Book, p. 415. and MS Ed. 34.

[p] N° 47. 51. 84.

[q] N° 93. 132. MS Ed. 37.

[r] Perhaps Turmerick. See ad loc.

[s] Ter. Andr. I. 1. where Donatus and Mad. Dacier explain it of Cooking. Mr. Hearne, in deſcribing our Roll, ſee above, p. xi, by an unaccountable miſtake, read *Fary* inſtead of *Cury*, the plain reading of the MS.

[t] Junii Etym. v. Diet.

Cooks

Cooks exprefsly tell us, in their proem, that their work was compiled ' by affent and avyfement of ' maifters of phifik and of philofophie that dwellid ' in his [the King's] court' where *phifik* is ufed in the fenfe of medecine, *phyficus* being applied to perfons profeffing the Art of Healing long before the 14th century [u], as implying *fuch* knowledge and fkill in all kinds of natural fubftances, conftituting the *materia medica*, as was neceffary for them in practice.   At the end of the Editor's MS. is written this rhyme,

Explicit coquina que eft optima medicina [x].

There is much relative to eatables in the *Schola Salernitana*; and we find it ordered, that a phyfician fhould over-fee the young prince's wet-nurfe at every meal, to infpect her meat and drink [y].

But after all the avyfement of phyficians and phi-lofophers, our proceffes do not appear by any means to be well calculated for the benefit of recipients, but rather inimical to them.   Many of them are fo highly feafoned, are fuch ftrange and heterogeneous

---

[u] Reginaldus Phificus. M. Paris, p. 410. 412. 573. 764.   Et in Vit. p. 94. 103. Chaucer's *Medicus* is a doctor of phifick, p. 4. V. Junii Etym. voce Phyfician.   For later times, v. J. Roffus, p. 93.

[x] That of Donatus is more modeft ' Culina medicinæ famulatrix ' eft.'

[y] Lel. Collect. IV. p. 183. ' Diod. Siculus refert primos Ægypti Reges victum quotidianum omnino fumpfiffe ex medicorum præ-fcripto.' Lifter ad Apic. p. ix.

I   compo-

compofitions, meer olios and gallimawfreys, that they
feem removed as far as poffible from the intention of
contributing to health ; indeed the meffes are fo re-
dundant and complex, that in regard to herbs, in
N° 6, no lefs than ten are ufed, where we fhould now
be content with two or three: and fo the fallad,
N° 76, confifts of no lefs than 14 ingredients. The
phyficians appear only to have taken care that nothing directly noxious was fuffered to enter the forms.
However, in the Editor's MS. N° 11, there is a
prefcription for making a *colys*, I prefume a *cullis*, or
invigorating broth ; for which fee Dodfley's Old Plays,
vol. II. 124. vol. V. 148. vol. VI. 355. and the
feveral plays mentioned in a note to the firft mentioned
paffage in the Edit. 1780 [z].

I obferve further, in regard to this point, that the
quantities of things are feldom fpecified [a], but are too
much left to the tafte and judgement of the cook,
who, if he fhould happen to be rafh and inconfide-
rate, or of a bad and undiftinguifhing tafte, was ca-
pable of doing much harm to the guefts, to invalids
efpecially.

Though the cooks at Rome, as has been already
noted, were amongft the loweft flaves, yet it was not
fo more anciently ; Sarah and Rebecca cook, and fo

[z] See alfo Lylie's Euphues, p. 282. Cavendifh, Life of Wolfey,
p. 151, where we have *callis*, malè; Cole's and Lyttleton's Dict.
and Junii Etymolog. v. Collice.

[a] See however, N° 191, and Editor's MS II. 7.

d   do

do Patroclus and Automedon in the ninth Iliad. It
were to be wifhed indeed, that the Reader could be
made acquainted with the names of our *mafter-cooks*,
but it is not in the power of the Editor to gratify him
in that; this, however, he may be affured of, that as
the Art was of confequence in the reign of Richard,
a prince renowned and celebrated in the Roll[b], for
the fplendor and elegance of his table, they muft
have been perfons of no inconfiderable rank : the
king's firft and fecond cooks are now efquires by their
office, and there is all the reafon in the world to believe they were of equal dignity heretofore[c]. To fay
a word of king *Richard:* he is faid in the proeme to
have been ' acōnted the beft and ryalleft vyand [cu-
' riofo in eating] of all eftē kynges.' This, however, muft reft upon the teftimony of our cooks, fince
it does not appear otherwife by the fuffrage of hiftory,
that he was particularly remarkable for his nicenefs
and delicacy in eating, like Heliogabalus, whofe
favourite difhes are faid to have been the tongues of
peacocks and nightingales, and the brains of parrots
and pheafants[d]; or like Sept. Geta, who, according
to Jul. Capitolinus[e], was fo curious, fo whimfical,
as to order the difhes at his dinners to confift of things
which all began with the fame letters. Sardanapalus

[b] Vide the proeme.

[c] See above.

[d] Univ. Hift. XV. p. 352. ' Æfopus pater linguas avium huma-
' na vocales lingua cænavit; filius margaritas.' Lifter ad Apicium,
p. vii.

[e] Jul. Capitolinus, c. 5.

again, as we have it in Athenæus [f], gave a *præmium* to any one that invented and ſerved him with ſome novel cate; and Sergius Orata built a houſe at the entrance of the Lucrine lake, purpoſely for the pleaſure and convenience of eating the oyſters perfectly freſh. Richard II. is certainly not repreſented in ſtory as reſembling any ſuch epicures, or capriccioſo's, as theſe [g]. It may, however, be fairly preſumed, that good living was not wanting among the luxuries of that effeminate and diſſipated reign.

My next obſervation is, that the meſſes both in the Roll and the Editor's MS, are chiefly ſoups, potages, ragouts, haſhes, and the like hotche-potches; entire joints of meat being never *ſerved*, and animals, whether fiſh or fowl, ſeldom brought to table whole, but hacked and hewed, and cut in pieces or gobbets [h]; the mortar alſo was in great requeſt, ſome meſſes being actually denominated from it, as *mortrews*, or *morterelys*, as in the Editor's MS. Now in this ſtate of things, the general mode of eating muſt either have been with the ſpoon or the fingers; and this perhaps may have been the reaſon that ſpoons be-

[f] Athenæus, lib. xii. c. 7. Something of the ſame kind is related of Heliogabalus, Liſter Præf. ad Apic. p. vii.

[g] To omit the paps of a pregnant ſow, Hor. I. Ep. xv. 40. where ſee Monſ. Dacier; Dr. Fuller relates, that the tongue of carps were accounted by the ancient Roman palate-men moſt delicious meat. Worth. in Suſſex. See other inſtances of extravagant Roman luxury in Liſter's Præf. to Apicius, p. vii.

[h] See, however, N° 33, 34, 35. 146.

came

came an ufual prefent from goffips to their god-chil-
dren at chriftenings [i]; and that the bafon and ewer,
for wafhing before and after dinner, was introduced,
whence the *ewerer* was a great officer [k], and the *ewery*
is retained at Court to this day [l]; we meet with *da-
mafke water* after dinner [m], I prefume, perfumed;
and the words *ewer*, &c. plainly come from the Saxon
eƿe, or French eau, *water*.

Thus, to return, in that little anecdote relative to
the Conqueror and William Fitz-Ofbern, mentioned
above, not the crane, but *the flefh of the crane* is faid
to have been under-roafted. Table, or cafe-knives,
would be of little ufe at this time [n], and the art of
carving fo perfectly ufelefs, as to be almoft unknown.
In about a century afterwards, however, as appears
from archbifhop Neville's entertainment, many articles were ferved whole, and lord Wylloughby was
the carver [o]. So that carving began now to be prac-

[i] The king, in Shakefpeare, Hen. VIII. act iv. fc. 2. and 3. calls
the gifts of the fponfors, *fpoons*. Thefe were ufually gilt, and, the
figures of the apoftles being in general carved on them, were called
apoftle fpoons. See Mr. Steevens's note in Ed. 1778, vol. VII. p. 312,
alfo Gent. Mag. 1768, p. 426.

[k] Lel. Collect. IV. p. 328. VI. p. 2.

[l] See Dr. Percy's curious notes on the Northumb. Book, p. 417.

[m] Ibid. VI. p. 5. 18.

[n] They were not very common at table among the Greeks. Cafaub.
ad Athenæum, col. 278. but fee Lel. Coll. VI. p. 7.

[o] Leland, Collectan. VI. p. 2. Archbifhop Warham alfo had his
carver, ibid. p. 18. See alfo, IV. p. 236. 240. He was a great
officer. Northumb. Book, p. 443.

tifed, and the proper terms devifed. Wynken de Worde printed a *Book of Kervinge*, A. 1508, wherein the faid terms are regiftered [p]. ' The ufe of *forks* ' at table, fays Dr. Percy, did not prevail in Eng- ' land till the reign of James I. as we learn from a ' remarkable paffage in *Coryat* [q]; the paffage is indeed curious, but too long to be here tranfcribed, where brevity is fo much in view; wherefore I fhall only add, that forks are not now ufed in fome parts of Spain [r]. But then it may be faid, what becomes of the old Englifh hofpitality in this cafe, the *roaft-beef of Old England,* fo much talked of? I anfwer, thefe bulky and magnificent difhes muft have been the product of later reigns, perhaps of queen Elizabeth's time, fince it is plain that in the days of Rich. II. our anceftors lived much after the French fafhion. As to hofpitality, the houfeholds of our Nobles were immenfe, officers, retainers, and fervants, being entertained almoft without number; but then, as appears from the Northumberland Book, and afterwards from the houfehold eftablifhment of the prince of Wales, A. 1610, the individuals, or at leaft fmall parties, had their *quantum,* or ordinary, ferved out, where any good œconomy was kept, apart to themfelves [s]. Again, we find in our Roll, that great quan-

---

[p] Ames, Typ. Ant. p. 90. The terms may alfo be feen in Rand. Holme III. p. 78.

[q] Dr. Percy, l. c.

[r] Thickneffe, Travels, p. 260.

[s] Dr. Birch, Life of Henry prince of Wales, p. 457. feq.

tities

tities of the refpective viands of the hafhes, were often made at once, as N° 17, *Take hennes or conynges.* 24, *Take hares.* 29, *Take pygges.* And 31, *Take gees,* &c. So that hofpitality and plentiful houfe-keeping could juft as well be maintained this way, as by the other of cumbrous unwieldy meffes, as much as a man could carry.

As the meffes and fauces are fo complex, and the ingredients confequentl fo various, it feems neceffary that a word fhould be fpoken concerning the principal of them, and fuch as are more frequently employed, before we pafs to our method of proceeding in the publication.

Butter is little ufed. 'Tis firft mentioned N° 81, and occurs but rarely after [t]; 'tis found but once in the Editor's MS, where it is written *boter.* The ufual fubftitutes for it are oil-olive and lard; the latter is frequently called *grees,* or *grece,* or *white-grece,* as N° 18. 193. *Capons in Greafe* occur in Birch's Life of Henry prince of Wales, p. 459, 460. and fee Lye in Jun. Etym. v. *Greafie.* Bifhop Patrick has a remarkable paffage concerning this article: ' Though we read of cheefe in *Homer, Euripides,* ' *Theocritus,* and others, yet they never mention ' *butter :* nor hath Ariftotle a word of it, though he ' hath fundry obfervations about cheefe : for butter

[t] N° 91, 92. 160.

' was

' was not a thing then known among the *Greeks*;
' though we fee by this and many other places, it was
' an ancient food among the eaftern people ᵘ.' The
Greeks, I prefume, ufed oil inftead of it, and butter
in fome places of fcripture is thought to mean only
cream ˣ.

Cheefe. See the laft article, and what is faid of
the old Britons above; as likewife our Gloffary.

Ale is applied, N° 113, et alibi; and often in the Editor's MS. as 6, 7, &c. It is ufed inftead of wine, N° 22,
and fometimes along with bread in the Editor's MS. ʸ
Indeed it is a current opinion that brewing with hops
was not introduced here till the reign of king
Henry VIII. ᶻ *Bere*, however, is mentioned A.
1504ª.

Wine is common, both red, and white, N° 21. 53.
37. This article they partly had of their own growth ᵇ,
and partly by importation from France ᶜ and Greece ᵈ.

ᵘ Bifhop Patrick on Genefis xviii. 8.
ˣ Calmet, v. Butter. So Judges iv. 19. compared with v. 25.
ʸ II. N° 13, 14, 15.
ᶻ Stow, Hift. p. 1038.
ª Lel. Coll. VI. p. 30. and fee Dr. Percy on Northumb. Book,
p. 414.
ᵇ Archæologia, I. p. 319. III. p. 53.
ᶜ Barrington's Obferv. on Statutes, p. 209. 252. Edit. 3d. Ar-
chæolog. I. p. 330. Fitz-Stephen, p. 33. Lel. Cell. VI. p. 14.
Northumb. Book, p. 6. and notes.
ᵈ N° 20. 64. 99.

They

They had alſo Rheniſh [e], and probably ſeveral other
ſorts. The *vynegreke* is among the ſweet wines in a
MS of Mr. Aſtle.

Rice. As this grain was but little, if at all, culti-
vated in England, it muſt have been brought from
abroad. Whole or ground rice enters into a large
number of our compoſitions, and *reſmolle*, N° 96, is a
direct preparation of it.

Alkenet. *Anchuſa* is not only uſed for colouring,
but alſo fried and yfondred, 62. yfondyt, 162. i. e.
diſſolved, or ground. 'Tis thought to be a ſpecies
of the *buglos*.

Saffron. Saffrwm, Brit. whence it appears, that
this name ran through moſt languages. Mr. Weever
informs us, that this excellent drug was brought hither
in the time of Edward III. [f] and it may be true; but
ſtill no ſuch quantity could be produced here in the
next reign as to ſupply that very large conſumption
which we ſee made of it in our Roll, where it occurs
not only as an ingredient in the proceſſes, but alſo is
uſed for colouring, for flouriſhing, or garniſhing. It
makes a yellow, N° 68, and was imported from Egypt,
or Cilicia, or other parts of the Levant, where the
Turks call it Safran, from the Arabic Zapheran,

---

[e] N° 99.
[f] Fun. Mon. p. 624.

whence

whence the English, Italians, French, and Germans, have apparently borrowed their respective names of it. The Romans were well acquainted with the drug, but did not use it much in the kitchen [g]. Pere Calmet says, the Hebrews were acquainted with anise, ginger, saffron, but no other spices [h].

Pynes. There is some difficulty in enucleating the meaning of this word, though it occurs so often. It is joined with dates, N° 20. 52. with honey clarified, 63. with powder-fort, saffron, and salt, 161. with ground dates, raisins, good powder, and salt, 186. and lastly they are fried, 38. Now the dish here is *morree*, which in the Editor's MS. 37, is made of mulberries (and no doubt has its name from them), and yet there are no mulberries in our dish, but pynes, and therefore I suspect, that mulberries and pynes are the same, and indeed this fruit has some resemblance to a pynecone. I conceive *pynnonade*, the dish, N° 51, to be so named from the pynes therein employed; and quære whether *pyner* mentioned along with powder-fort, saffron, and salt, N° 155, as above in N° 161, should not be read *pynes*. But, after all, we have cones brought hither from Italy full of nuts, or kernels, which upon roasting come out of their *capsulæ*, and are much eaten by the common people, and these perhaps may be the thing intended.

[g] Dr. Lister, Præf. ad Apicium, p. xii.
[h] Calmet. Dict. v. Eating.

Honey

Honey was the great and univerfal fweetner in remote antiquity, and particularly in this ifland, where it was the chief conftituent of *mead* and *metheglin*. It is faid, that at this day in *Paleſtine* they ufe honey in the greateſt part of their ragouts [i]. Our cooks had a method of clarifying it, N° 18. 41. which was done by putting it in a pot with whites of eggs and water, beating them well together; then fetting it over the fire, and boiling it; and when it was ready to boil over to take it and cool it, N° 59. This I prefume is called *clere honey*, N° 151. And, when honey was fo much in ufe, it appears from Barnes that *refining* it was a trade of itfelf [k].

Sugar, or Sugur [l], was now beginning here to take place of honey; however, they are ufed together, N° 67. Sugar came from the Indies, by way of Damafcus and Aleppo, to Venice, Genoa, and Pifa, and from thefe laſt places to us [m]. It is here not only frequently ufed, but was of various forts, as *cypre*, N° 41. 99. 120. named probably from the ifle of Cyprus, whence it might either come directly to us, or where it had received fome improvement by way of refining. There is mention of *blanch-powder or*

[i] Calmet. Dict. v. Meats.
[k] Barnes, Hiſt. of E. III. p. 111.
[l] N° 70, Edi·or's MS. 17. alibi.
[m] Moll, Geogr. II. p. 130. Harris, Coll. of Voyages, I. p. 874. Ed. Campbell.

white

white sugar, 132. They, however, were not the same, for see N° 193. Sugar was clarified sometimes with wine [n].

Spices. *Species*. They are mentioned in general N° 133, and *whole spices*, 167, 168. but they are more commonly specified, and are indeed greatly used, though being imported from abroad, and from so far as Italy or the Levant (and even there must be dear), some may wonder at this: but it should be considered, that our Roll was chiefly compiled for the use of noble and princely tables; and the same may be said of the Editor's MS. The spices came from the same part of the world, and by the same route, as sugar did. The *spicery* was an ancient department at court, and had its proper officers.

As to the particular sorts, these are,

Cinamon. *Canèll*. 14. 191. *Canel*, Editor's MS. 10. *Kanell*, ibid. 32. is the Italian *Canella*. See Chaucer. We have the flour or powder, N° 20. 62. See Wiclif. It is not once mentioned in Apicius.

Macys, 14. 121. Editor's MS. 10. *Maces*, 134. Editor's MS. 27. They are used whole, N° 158. and are always expressed plurally, though we now use the singular, *mace*. See Junii Etym.

[n] N° 20. 148.

Clove .

Cloves. N° 20. Diſhes are flouriſhed with them, 22. 158. Editor's MS. 10. 27. where we have *clowys gylofres*, as in our Roll, N° 194. *Powdour gylofre* occurs 65. 191. Chaucer has *clowe* in the ſingular, and ſee him v. Clove-gelofer.

Galyngal, 30. and elſewhere. Galangal, the long rooted cyperus°, is a warm cardiac and cephalic. It is uſed in powder,. 30. 47. and was the chief ingredient in *galentine*, which, I think, took its name from it.

Pepper. It appears from Pliny that this pungent, warm ſeaſoning, ſo much in eſteem at Rome°, came from the Eaſt Indies°, and, as we may ſuppoſe, by way of Alexandria. We obtained it no doubt, in the 14th century, from the ſame quarter, though not exactly by the ſame route, but by Venice or Genoa. It is uſed both whole, N° 35, and in powder, N° 83. And long-pepper occurs, if we read the place rightly, in N° 191.

Ginger, gyngyn. 64. 136. alibi. Powder is uſed, 17. 20. alibi. and Rabelais IV. c. 59. the white

---

° Gloſſary to Chaucer. See the Northumb. Book, p. 415 and 19. alſo Quincy's Diſpenſ. and Brookes's Nat. Hiſt. of Vegetables.

° Liſter, Præf. ad Apicium, p. xii.

° Plinius, Nat. Hiſt. XII. cap. 7.

powder, 131. and it is the name of a mefs, 139. quære whether *gyngyn* is not mifread for *gyngyr*, for fee Junii Etym. The Romans had their ginger from Troglodytica [r].

Cubebs, 64, 121. are a warm fpicy grain from the eaft.

Grains of Paradice, or *de parys*, 137. [s] are the greater cardamoms.

Noix mufcadez, 191. nutmegs.

The caraway is once mentioned, N° 53. and was an exotic from *Caria*, whence, according to Mr. Lye, it took its name : ' funt femina, inquit, *carri* vel *carrei*, ' fic dicti a Caria, ubi copiofiffimè nafcitur [t].'

Powder-douce, which occurs fo often, has been thought by fome, who have juft peeped into our Roll, to be the fame as fugar, and only a different name for it ; but they are plainly miftaken, as is evident from 47. 51. 164. 165. where they are mentioned together as different things. In fhort, I take powder-douce to be either powder of galyngal, for fee Editor's MS II. 20. 24, or a compound made of fundry

---

[r] Bochart. III. col. 332.
[s] See our Gloff. voce Greynes.
[t] Lye, in Junii Etymolog.

aromatic

aromatic ſpices ground or beaten ſmall, and kept always ready at hand in ſome proper receptacle. It is otherwiſe termed *good powders,*. 83. 130. and in Editor's MS 17. 37. 38 ᵘ. or *powder* ſimply, Nº 169, 170. *White powder-douce* occurs Nº 51, which ſeems to be the ſame as blanch-powder, 132. 193. called *blaynſhe powder*, and bought ready prepared, in Northumb. Book, p. 19. It is ſometimes uſed with powder-fort, 38. 156. for which ſee the next and laſt article.

Powder-fort, 10. 11. ſeems to be a mixture likewiſe of the warmer ſpices, pepper, ginger, &c. pulverized.: hence we have *powder-fort of gynger, other of canel*, 14. It is called *ſtrong powder*, 22. and perhaps may ſometimes be intended by *good powders.* If you will ſuppoſe it to be kept ready prepared by the vender, it may be the *powder-marchant*, 113. 118. found joined in two places with powder-douce. This Speght ſays is what gingerbread is made of ; but Skinner diſapproves this explanation, yet, ſays Mr. Urry, gives none of his own.

After thus travelling through the moſt material and moſt uſed ingredients, the *ſpykenard de ſpayn* occurring only once, I ſhall beg leave to offer a few words on the nature, and in favour of the preſent publication, and the method employed in the proſecution of it.

ᵘ But ſee the next article.

The

·ffor to make malmenny·

xx. xvij.

Take ye brede and of fleyssh of capons or of hennys þ flessh smale and grynde hem smale in a morter take mylke of almandis wt ye þ broþ of freyssh begͤ of freyssh flessh & put þe flessh i þ mylke of in þe broþ and set hem to þ fyre & take hem wt flo of ryse caftdon or amydon as chargeaūt as þ blanke defire & ȝe þolk of eyren and saffron for to make hit ȝelow and whan it is grytt in gyfbȝ of blank soñ aȝe a bone caȝȝo so alȝȝo & þaȝȝe powȝ of saffrngale aboue and þre it forþ

The common language of the *formulæ*, though old and obfolete, as naturally may be expected from the age of the MS, has no other difficulty in it but what may eafily be overcome by a fmall degree of practice and application [x] : however, for the further illuftration of this matter, and the fatisfaction of the curious, a *fac fimile* of one of the recipes is reprefented in the annexed plate. If here and there a hard and uncouth term or expreffion may occur, fo as to ftop or embarrafs the lefs expert, pains have been taken to explain them, either in the annotations under the text, or in the Index and Gloffary, for we have given it both titles, as intending it fhould anfwer the purpofe of both [y]. Now in forming this alphabet, as it would have been an endlefs thing to have recourfe to all our gloffaries, now fo numerous, we have confined ourfelves, except perhaps in fome few inftances, in which the authorities are always mentioned, to certain contemporary writers, fuch as the Editor's MS, of which we fhall fpeak more particularly hereafter, Chaucer, and Wiclif; with whom we have affociated Junius' Etymologicon Anglicanum.

[x] Doing, hewing, hacking, grynding, kerving, &c. are eafily underftood.

[y] By combining the Index and Gloffary together, we have had an opportunity of elucidating fome terms more at large than could conveniently be done in the notes. We have alfo caft the Index to the Roll, and that to the Editor's MS, into one alphabet; diftinguifhing, however, the latter from the former.

As

As the abbreviations of the Roll are here retained, in order to eſtabliſh and confirm the age of it, it has been thought proper to adopt the types which our printer had projećted for Domeſday-Book, with which we find that our charaćters very nearly coincide.

The names of the diſhes and ſauces have occaſioned the greateſt perplexity. Theſe are not only many in number, but are often ſo horrid and barbarous, to our ears at leaſt, as to be inveloped in ſeveral inſtances in almoſt impenetrable obſcurity. Biſhop Godwin complains of this ſo long ago as 1616[z]. The *Contents* prefixed will exhibit at once a moſt formidable liſt of theſe hideous names and titles, ſo that there is no need to report them here. A few of theſe terms the Editor humbly hopes he has happily enucleated, but ſtill, notwithſtanding all his labour and pains, the argument is in itſelf ſo abſtruſe at this diſtance of time, the helps ſo few, and his abilities in this line of knowledge and ſcience ſo ſlender and confined, that he fears he has left the far greater part of the taſk for the more ſagacious reader to ſupply: indeed, he has not the leaſt doubt, but other gentlemen of curioſity in ſuch matters (and this publication is intended for them alone) will be ſo happy as to clear up ſeveral difficulties, which appear now to him inſuperable. It muſt be confeſſed again, that

---

[z] Godwin de Præſul. p. 684.

the

the Editor may probably have often failed in thofe very points, which he fancies and flatters himfelf to have elucidated, but this he is willing to leave to the candour of the public.

Now in regard to the helps I mentioned ; there is not much to be learnt from the Great Inthronization-feaft of archbifhop Robert Winchelfea, A. 1295, even if it were his ; but I rather think it belongs to archbifhop William Warham, A. 1504 [a]. Some ufe, however, has been made of it.

Ralph Bourne was inftalled abbot of St. Auguftine's, near Canterbury, A. 1309 ; and William Thorne has inferted a lift of provifions bought for the feaft, with their prices, in his Chronicle [b].

The Great Feaft at the Inthronization of George Nevile archbifhop of York, 6 Edward IV. is printed by Mr. Hearne [c], and has been of good fervice.

[a] In Dr. Drake's edition of archbifhop Parker, p. lxiii. it is given to archbifhop Winchelfea: but fee Mr. Battely's Append. to *Cantuaria Sacra*, p. 27. or the Archæologia, I. p. 330. and Leland's Collectanea, VI. p. 30. where it is again printed, and more at large, and afcribed to Warham.

[b] Thorne, Chron. inter X Script. Col. 2010. or Lel. Collect. VI. p. 34. Ed. 1770.

[c] Leland, Collect. VI. p. 2. See alfo Randle Holme, III. p. 77. Bifhop Godwin de Præful. p. 695. Ed. Richardfon; where there are fome confiderable variations in the meffes or fervices, and he and the Roll in Leland will correct one another.

Elizabeth,

Elizabeth, queen of king Henry VII. was crowned A. 1487, and the meſſes at the dinner, in two courſes, are regiſtered in the late edition of Leland's Collectenea, A. 1770 [d], and we have profited thereby.

The Lenten Inthronization-feaſt of archbiſhop William Warham, A. 1504 [e], given us at large by Mr. Hearne [f], has been alſo conſulted.

There is a large catalogue of viands in Rabelais, lib. iv. cap. 59. 60., And the Engliſh tranſlation of Mr. Ozell affording little information, I had recourſe to the French original, but not to much more advantage.

There is alſo a Royal Feaſt at the wedding of the earl of Devonſhire, in the Harleian Miſc. N° 279, and it has not been neglected.

Randle Holme, in his multifarious *Academy of Armory*, has an alphabet of terms and diſhes [g]; but though I have preſſed him into the ſervice, he has not contributed much as to the more difficult points.

The Antiquarian Repertory, vol. II. p. 211, exhibits an entertainment of the mayor of Rocheſter, A. 1460; but there is little to be learned from thence. The preſent work was printed before N° 31 of the Antiquarian Repertory, wherein ſome ancient recipes in Cookery are publiſhed, came to the Editor's hand.

[d] Vol. IV. p. 226.
[e] See firſt paragraph before.
[f] Leland's Collect. VI. p. 16.
[g] Holme, Acad. of Armory, III. p. 81.

I muſt

I muſt not omit my acknowledgments to my learned friend the preſent dean of Carliſle, to whom I ſtand indebted for his uſeful notes on the Northumberland-Houſehold Book, as alſo for the book itſelf.

Our chief aſſiſtance, however, has been drawn from a MS belonging to the Editor, denoted, when cited, by the ſignature *MS. Ed.* It is a vellum miſcellany in ſmall quarto, and the part reſpecting this ſubject conſiſts of ninety-one Engliſh recipes (or *nyms*) in cookery. Theſe are diſpoſed into two parts, and are intituled, ' Hic incipiunt univerſa ſervicia tam de ' carnibus quam de piſſibus.' ʰ The ſecond part, relates to the dreſſing of fiſh, and other lenten fare, though forms are alſo there intermixed which properly belong to fleſh-days. This leads me to obſerve, that both here, and in the Roll, meſſes are ſometimes accommodated, by making the neceſſary alterations, both to fleſh and fiſh-days. ⁱ Now, though the ſubjects of the MS are various, yet the hand-writing is uniform ; and at the end of one of the tracts is added, ' Explicit maſſa Compoti, Anno Dñi Mˡᵒ CCCᵐᵒ ' octogeſimo primo ipſo die Felicis et Audacti.' ᵏ, i. e. 30 Aug. 1381, in the reign of Rich. II. The language and orthography accord perfectly well with this date, and the collection is conſequently contemporary with our Roll, and was made chiefly, though

ʰ It is *piſſibus* again in the title to the Second Part.

ⁱ Nᵒ 7. 84. here Nᵒ 17. 35. 97.

ᵏ In the common calendars of our miſſals and breviaries, the latter ſaint is called *Adauctus*, but in the Kalend. Roman. of Joh. Fronto, Paris 1652, p. 126, he is written *Audactus*, as here; and ſee Martyrolog. Bedæ, p. 414.

not altogether, for the ufe of great tables, as appears from the *fturgeon*, and the great quantity of venifon therein prefcribed for.

As this MS is fo often referred to in the annotations, gloffary, and even in this preface, and is a compilation of the fame date, on the fame fubject, and in the fame language, it has been thought advifeable to print it, and fubjoin it to the Roll; and the rather, becaufe it really furnifhes a confiderable enlargement on the fubject, and exhibits many forms unnoticed in the Roll.

To conclude this tedious preliminary detail, though unqueftionably a moft neceffary part of his duty, the Editor can fcarcely forbear laughing at himfelf, when he reflects on his paft labours, and recollects thofe lines of the poet Martial ;

Turpe eft difficiles habere nugas,

Et ftultus labor eft ineptiarum.   II. 86.

and that poffibly mefdames *Carter* and *Raffald*, with twenty others, might have far better acquitted themfelves in the adminiftration of this province, than he has done.   He has this comfort and fatisfaction, however, that he has done his beft; and that fome confiderable names amongft the learned, Humelbergius, Torinus, Barthius, our countryman Dr. Lifter, Almeloveen, and others, have beftowed no lefs pains in illuftrating an author on the fame fubject, and fcarcely of more importance, the *Pfeudo-Apicius*.

3   T H E

THE

FORME of CURY.

... fome ᵃ of cury ᵇ was compiled of the chef Maiſt⁹ Cok⁹ of kyng Richard the Secunde kyng of . nglond ᶜ aftir the Conqueſt. the which was acoñted þ̇ ᵈ beſt and ryalleſt vyand ᵉ of alle cſtē . yng⁹ f and it was cōpiled by aſſent and

---

ᵃ This is a kind of Preamble to the Roll. A ſpace is left for the initial word, intended to be afterwards written in red ink, and preſumed to be Ðis. *Fome*, the *lineola* over it being either caſually omitted, or ſince obliterated, means *form*, written Fŏme below, and in Nº 195.

ᵇ Cury. Cookery. We have adopted it in the Title. V. Preface.

ᶜ ynglond. *E* was intended to be prefixed in red ink. Vide Note ᵃ and f.

ᵈ þ. This Saxon letter with the power of *th*, is uſed almoſt perpetually in our Roll and the Editor's Mſ. Every one may not have adverted to it; but this character is the ground of our preſent abbreviations ẏ the, ẏ that, ẏ this, &c. the y in theſe caſes being evidently only an altered and more modern way of writing þ.

ᵉ vyānd. This word is to be underſtood in the concrete, *quaſi* vyander, a curious epicure, an *Apicius*. V. Preface.

f cſtē ynges. Chriſtian kings. *K* being to be inferted afterwards (v. note ᵃ and ᶜ) in red ink. Chaucer, v. chriſten.

A

avyſe-

avyſement of Maiſters and ^g phiſik ^h and of philoſophie þaꞇ dwellid in his court. Firſt it techiþ a man for to make cōmune potages and cōmune meetis for howſhold as þey ſhold be made craftly and holſomly. Aftirward it techiþ for to make curious potages ⁊ meet and ſotiltees ⁱ for alle manē of States bothe hye and lowe. And the techyng of the fōme of making of potages ⁊ of meet bothe of fleſsh and of fiſsh. buth ^k y ſette here by noumbre and by ordre. ſſo þis little table here ſewyng ^l wole teche a man with oute taryyng: to fynde what meete þ̆ hym luſt for to have.

^g and. Read *of*.

^h Phiſik. V. Preface.

ⁱ Sotiltees. Devices in paſte, wax, and confeƈtionary ware; reviving now, in ſome meaſure, in our grander deſerts. V. Index.

^k buth. *Be*, or *are*. V. Index.

^l ſewing. Following; from the French. Hence our *enſue* written formerly *enſew*. Skelton, p. 144; and *enfiew*, Ames Typ. Ant. p, 9.

^m F is omitted for the reaſon given in note ².

hebolas.

Chikens

[n] Nº II. XX. II. is omitted.

Chyryfe.

Sauſe

S auſe Sarzyne. . . . . ɪɪɪɪ. ɪɪɪɪ.
                            xx.

c reme of almānd. . . . . ɪɪɪɪ. v.
                            xx.

G rewel of almand. . . . . ɪɪɪɪ. vɪ.
                            xx.

c awdel of almand mylk. . . . . ɪɪɪɪ. vɪɪ.
                            xx.

I owt of almand mylk. . . . . ɪɪɪɪ. vɪɪɪ.
                            xx.

f ygey. . . . . ɪɪɪɪ. ɪx.
                            xx.

P ochee. . . . . ɪɪɪɪ. x.
                            xx.

b rewet of ayrēn. . . . . ɪɪɪɪ. xɪ.
                            xx.

M acrows. . . . . ɪɪɪɪ. xɪɪ.
                            xx.

t oſtee. . . . . ɪɪɪɪ. xɪɪɪ.
                            xx.

G yndawdry. . . . . ɪɪɪɪ. xɪɪɪɪ.
                            xx.

e rbowle. . . . . ɪɪɪɪ. xv.
                            xx.

R eſmolle. . . . . ɪɪɪɪ. xvɪ.
                            xx.

v yannde.Cipre. . . . . ɪɪɪɪ. xvɪɪ.
                            xx.

V yañde Cipre of Samon. . . . . . . ɪɪɪɪ. xvɪɪɪ.
                            xx.

v yañde Ryal. . . . . ɪɪɪɪ. ɪx.

C ompoſt. . . . . c.

g elee of Fyſsh. . . . . c. ɪ.

G elee of fleſsh. . . . . c. ɪɪ.

C hyſanne. . . . . c. ɪɪɪ.

c. ongur in ſawce. . . . . c. ɪɪɪɪ.

R ygh in ſawce. . . . . c. v.

m akerel in ſawce. . . . . c. vɪ.

P ykes in braſey. . . . . c. vɪɪ.

p orpeys in broth. . . . . c. vɪɪɪ.

B allok broth. . . . . c. ɪx.

                              eles

ſawce

ſ awce blanche for Capoñs y ſode. . . VI. XVI.

S awce Noyre for Capons y roſted. . . VI. XVII.

g alentyne. . . . . VI. XVIII.

G yngeñ. . . . . VI. XIX.

v erde ſawſe. . . . . VII.

S awce Noyre for malard. . . . . . VII. I.

c awdęl for Gees. . . . . VII. II.

C hawdōn for Swann. . . . . VII. III.

ſ awce Camelyne. . . . . VII. IIII.

L umbard Muſtard. . . . . VII. V.

n ota. . . . . VII. VI.

N ota. . . . . VII. VII.

ſ rytō blañched. . . . . VII. VIII.

F rytō of paſtñak.. . . . . VII. IX.

ſ rytō of mylke. . . . . VII. X.

ſ rytō of Erbes. . . . . VII. XI.

r aiſiowls. . . . . VII. XII.

W hyte milat. . . . . VII. XIII.

c ruſtard of fleſh. . . . . VII. XIIII.

M ylat of Pork. . . . . VII. XV.

c ruſtard of Fyſh. . . . . VII. XVI.

C ruſtard of erbis on fyſsh day. . . . VII. XVII.

l eſsh fryed in lentōn. . . . . . . VII. XVIII.

W aſtels y farced. . . . . VII. XIX.

ſ awge y farced. . . . . VIII.

S awgeat . . . . VIII. I.

cryſpes.

B   comadoꝛ

Ɛplicit tabula.

For to make gronden Benes [a]. I.

TAKE benes and dry hē ī a noſt [b] or in an Ovene
and hulle hē wele and wyndewe [c] out þ hulk
and wayſhe hē clene ā do hē to ſeeþ in gode broth [d]
ā ete hē w Bacon.

For to make drawen Benes. II.

Take benes and ſeeþ hē and grynde hem ī a mortē [e]
and drawe hem up [f] w gode broth ā do Oynoñs in
the broth grete mynced [g] ā do þ to and colō it with
Safroñ and ſerve it forth.

---

[a] Grōnden Benes. Beans ground (y grōnd, as Nº 27. 53. 105.)
ſtript of their hulls. This was a diſh of the poorer houſeholder,
as alſo is 4 and 5, and ſome others.

[b] a noſt. An oſt, or kiln. Vide Gloſſ. *voce* Oſt.

[c] wyndewe. Winnow.

[d] gode broth. Prepared beforehand.

[e] mort'. Mortar.

[f] drawen hem up. Mix them.

[g] grete mynced. Groſsly, not too ſmall.

For to make grewel forced [h].   III.

Take grewel and do to the fyre with gode flefsh and
feeþ it wel. take the lire [i] of Pork and grynd it fmal [k]
and drawe the grewel thurgh a Stynõ [l] and colõ it wiþ
Safroñ and ſue [m] forth.

Caboches [n] in Potage.   IIII.

Take Caboch and quart hē and feeth hem in gode
broth with Oynoñs y mynced and the whyte of Lekes
y flyt and corue fmale [o] and do þ to fafroñ ā falt and
force it w̃ powdõ douce [p].

Rapes [q] in Potage.   V.

Take rapus and make hē clene and waifsh hē clene.
quare hem [r]. þboile hē. take hem up. caft hem in a
gode broth and feeþ hē. mynce Oynoñs and caft þ to

---

[h] forced, farced, enriched with flefh.   Vide Gloff.
[i] lire.   Flefh.
[k] grynd it fmal.   Bruife or beat in a mortar.
[l] ftȳno'.   Strainer.
[m] ſue.   Serve.   Vide Gloff.
[n] Caboches.   Probably cabbages.
[o] corue fmale.   Cut fmall.   V. *i corue* in Glof.
[p] powdõ douce.   Sweet aromatic powder.   V. Pref.
[q] Rapes, or rapus.   Turneps.
[r] quare hem.   Cut them in *fquares*, or fmall pieces.   V. Gloff.

Safroñ

Safron̄ and Salt̄ and meſſe it forth with powdŏ douce.
In the wiſe ˢ make of Paſturnak̊ ᵗ and skyrwat̊ ᵘ.

Eowt̊ ˣ of Fleſsh.   VI.

Take Borage. cool ʸ. langdebef ᶻ. pſel ᵃ. bet̊. orage ᵇ.
auance ᶜ. violet ᵈ. ſaẘay ᵉ. and fenkel ᶠ. and whane
þey buth ſode: preſſe hem wel ſmale. caſt hem in gode
broth ā ſeeþ hē. and ſūe hem forth.

Hebolace ᵍ.   VII.

Take Oynon̄s and erbes and hewe hem ſmall and
do þ̊ to gode broth. and aray ʰ it as þ̊ dideſt caboch̊.

ˢ in the wiſe, *i. e.* in the ſame manner. *Self* or *ſame*, ſeems to be
caſually omitted. Vide N° 11 and 122.

ᵗ Paſturnakes, for parſnips or carrots. V. Gloſſ.

ᵘ ſkyrwates, for ſkirrits or ſkirwicks.

ˣ Eowtes. *Lowtes*, N° 88, where, in the proceſs, it is *Rowtes*.
Quære the meaning, as Roots does not apply to the matter of the
Recipe. In N° 73 it is written *owtes*.   ʸ Cole, or colewort.

ᶻ Langdebef. Bugloſs, bugloſſum ſylveſtre. Theſe names all
ariſe from a ſimilitude to an ox's tongue. V. Mſ. Ed. N° 43.

ᵃ Perſel. Parſley.

ᵇ orage. Orach, *Atriplex.* Miller, Gard. Dict.

ᶜ auance. Fortè Avens. V. Avens, in Gloſſ.

ᵈ The leaves probably, and not the flower.

ᵉ Savory.   ᶠ Fenkel. Fennil.

ᵍ Hebolace. Contents, Hebolas; for *Herbolas*, from the herbs,
uſed; or, if the firſt letter be omitted (ſee the Contents), *Che-
bolas*, from the Chibols employed.

ʰ aray. Dreſs, ſet it out.

If þey be in fyſh day. make [i] on the ſame manē [k] with waͯ and oyle. and if it be not in Lent alye [l] it with zolkes of Eyren [m]. and dreſſe it forth and caſt þͨ to powdoͧ douce.

Gourdes in Potage.   VIII.

Take young Gowrdͨ pare hem and kerue [n] hem on pecys. caſt hem in gode broth. and do þͨ to a gode ptye [o] of Oynōs mynced. take Pork ſoden. grynd it and alye it þͨ wͭ and wiþ zolkes of ayrē. do þͨ to ſafrō and ſalt. and meſſe it forth with powdoͧ douce.

Ryſe [p] of Fleſh.   IX.

Take Ryſe and waiſhe hem clene. and do hē in erthen pot with gode broth and lat hem ſeeþ wel. afterward take Almānd mylke [q] and do þͨ to. and coloͧ it wiþ ſafrō ā ſalt. ā meſſe forth.

Funges [r].   X.

Take Funges and pare hem clene and dyce hem [s]. take leke and ſhred hym ſmall and do hy̅ to ſeeþ

---

[i] make. Dreſs. Vide Gloſſ.   [k] man̆e. manner.
[l] alye. Mix. V. Gloſſ.   [m] Eyren. Eggs. V. Gloſſ.
[n] kerve. Cut.   [o] p'tye. Party, i. e. quantity.
[p] Ryſe. Rice. V. Gloſſ.   [q] Almand mylke. V. Gloſſ.
[r] Funges. Muſhrooms.
[s] dyce hem. Cut them in ſquares. Vide *quare* in Gloſſ.

in gode broth. colo͛ it with ſafron and do þꝰ inne powdō fort [t].

Burſen [u]. XI.

Take the whyte of Lekꝰ. ſlype hem and ſhrede hem ſmall. take Noumblꝰ [x] of ſwyne and ꝑboyle hem in broth and wyne. take hym up and dreſſe hȳ and do the Leke in the broth. ſeeþ and do the Noumblꝰ þꝰ to make a Lyo͛ [y] of brode blode and vynegre and do þꝰ to Powdo͛ fort ſeeþ Oynōns mynce hem and do þꝰ to. the ſelf wiſe make of Piggꝰ.

Corat [z]. XII.

Take the Noumblꝰ of Calf. Swyne. or of Shepe. ꝑboile hem and ſkerꝑe hem to dyce [a]. caſt hem in gode broth and do þꝰ to erbes. grynde chyballꝰ [b]. ſmale y hewe. ſeeþ it tendre and lye it with zolkes of cyren̄. do þꝰ to vꝰious [c] ſafron̄ powdo͛ douce and ſalt. and ſ̄ue it forth.

[t] Powdō fort. Vide Preface.

[u] Burſen. Qu. the etymon.

[x] Noumbles. Entrails. V. Gloſſ.

[y] Lyo', Lyour. A mixture. Vide *alye* in Gloſſ.

[z] Corat. Qu.

[a] kerve hem to dyce. V. *quare* in Gloſſ.

[b] Chyballes. Chibols, young onions. V. Gloſſ.

[c] v'ious. Verjuice.

Noumbles.

Noumbles. XIII.

Take noumbl⁹ of Deer oþ ᵈ of oþ beeſt pboile hem
kerf hem to dyce. take the ſelf broth or better. take
brede and grynde with the broth. and temp it ᵉ up
with a gode qn̄tite of vyneḡ and wyne. take the oynon̄s
and pboyle hem. and mynce hem ſmale and do þ to.
colo̷ it with blode and do þ to powdō fort and ſalt
and boyle it wele and ſūe it fort ᶠ.

Roo ᵍ broth. XIIII.

Take the lire of the Deer oþ of the Roo pboile it
on ſmale peces. ſeeþ it wel half in waт̄ and half in
wyne. take brede and bray it wiþ the ſelf broth and
drawe blode þ to and lat it ſeeth to gedre w̄ powdō
fort of gynḡ oþ of canell ᵇ. and macys ⁱ. with a grete
porciōn of vineḡ with Raysōns of Corānte ᵏ.

ᵈ oþ. Other, i. e. or.
ᵉ temp it. Temper it, i. e. mix it.
ᶠ fort. Miſwritten for *forth*. So again N° 31. 127.
ᵍ Roo. Roe. The Recipe in Mſ. Ed. N° 53. is very different.
ʰ Canell. Cinnamon.
ⁱ macys. Mace. V. Preface and Gloſſ.
ᵏ Raysōns of Corānte. Currants. V. Gloſſ.

Tredure.

Tredure [1].   XV.

Take Brede and grate it. make a lyre [m] of rawe
ayren and do þto Safron and powdo douce. and lye
it up [n] w gode broth. and make it as a Cawdel. and
do þto a lytel vions.

Monchelet [o].   XVI.

Take Veel oþ Moton and fmite it to gobett feeþ it
i gode broth. caft þto erbes yhewe [p] gode wyne.
and a qntite of Oynons mynced. Powdo fort and Safron. and alye it w ayren and vions. but lat not feeþ
aft.

Bukkenade [q].   XVII.

Take Henn [r] oþ Conyng [s] oþ Veel oþ oþ Flefsh a
hewe hem to gobett waifche it and hit well [t]. grynde

---

[1] Tredure. A Cawdle; but quære the etymon. The French
tres dure does not feem to anfwer.

[m] lyre. Mixture.

[n] lye it up. Mix it.

[o] Monchelet. *Monchelet*, Contents.

[p] y hewe. Shred.

[q] Bukkenade. Vide Nº 118. qu.

[r] Hennes ; including, I fuppofe, chicken and pullets.

[s] Conynges. Coneys, Rabbits.

[t] hit well. This makes no fenfe, unlefs *hit* fignifies fmite or
beat.

Almand

Almand unblanched. and drawe hem up w þ broth cast þ inne rayſons of Corance. ſug. Powdo gyng erbes yſtewed in grees ᵘ. Oynoñs and Salt. If it is to to ˣ thynne. alye it up w flo of ryſe oþ· with oþ thyng and colo it with Safroñ.

Connat ʸ.   xviii.

Take Connes and pare hē. pyke out the beſt and do hem in a pot of erthe. do þto whyte grece þ he ſtewe þ inne. and lye hem up with hony clarified and with rawe zolk ᶻ and with a lytell almañd mylke and do þinne powdo fort and Safron. and loke þat it be yleeſshed ᵃ.

Drepee ᵇ.   xix.

Take blanched Almand grynde hem and temp hē up with gode broth take Oynoñs a grete qñtite pboyle hē and frye hē and do þto. take ſmale brydd ᶜ pboyle hē and do þto Pellydore ᵈ and ſalt. and· a lytel grece.

ᵘ Grees. Fat, lard, *grece*. Nº 19.

ˣ to to. So again, Nº 124   To is *too*, v. Gloſſ. And *too* is found doubled in this manner in *Mirrour for Magiſtrates*, p. 277. 371, and other authors.

ʸ Connat ſeems to be a kind of marmalade of connes, or quinces, from Fr. *Coing*. Chaucer, v. Coines. Written qnces Nº 30.

ᶻ Yolkes, i. e. of Eggs.

ᵉ yleeſshed. V. Gloſſ.   ᵇ Drepee. Qu.

ᵂ bryddes. Birds. *Per metathesin*; *v.* R. *in Indice.*

ᵈ Pellydore. Perhaps *pellitory*. *Peletour*, 104.

Maw-

Mawmenee [c].   XX.

Take a pottel of wyne greke. and ii. poñde of
fuᵍ take and clarifye the fuᵍ with a q̃ntite of wyne ã
drawe it thurgh a ſtỹnõ in to a pot of erthe take
flõ of Canell [f]. and medle [g] with ſũ of the wyne ã caſt
to gydre. take pyn [b] with Dat and frye hẽ a litell ĩ
grece oþ in oyle and caſt hẽ to gydre. take clowes [i] ã
flõ of canel hool [k] and caſt þto. take powdõ gyng̃.
canel. clow. colõ it with ſãndres a lytel yf hit be nede
caſt ſalt þto. and lat it ſeeþ warly [l] with a ſlowe fyre
and not to thyk [m], take brawñ [n] of Capoñs yteyſed [o].
oþ of Feſãnt teyſed ſmall and caſt þto.

---

[c] Vide Nᵒ 194, where it is called *Mawmenny.*

[f] Flour of Canell.   Powder of Cinamon.

[g] medle.   Mix.

[h] pynes.   A nut, or fruit.   Vide Gloſſ.

[i] clowes.   Cloves.

[k] hool.   Whole.   How can it be the flour, or powder, if whole?
Quære, *flower* of cand for *mace.*

[l] warly.   Warily, gently.

[m] not to thyk.   So as to be too thick; or perhaps, *not to thicken.*

[n] brawn.   Fleſhy part.   Few Capons are cut now except about
Darking in Surry; they have been excluded by the turkey, a more
magnificent, but perhaps not a better fowl.

[o] yteyſed, or *teyſed*, as afterwards.   Pulled in pieces by the fingers, called *teezing* Nᵒ 36.   This is done now with fleſh of turkeys,
and thought better than mincing.   Vide Junius, voce *Teaſe.*

Egurdouce ᵖ.   XXI.

Take Conyng̓ or Kydde and ſmyte hem on pecys
rawe. and frye hem in white grece. take rayſoñs of
Corañce and fry hē take oynoñs ꝑboile hem and hewe
hem ſmall and fry hem. take rede wyne ſug̓ w̄ᵗ powdõ
of pep. of gyng̓ of canel. ſalt. and caſt Ꝓto. and lat
it ſeeþ with a gode q̄ntite of white grece ā ſ̄ue it
forth.

Caponṡ in Coñcȳ �۹.   XXII.

Take Capons and roſt hem right hoot þat þey be
not half y nouhꝣ and hewe hem to gobett and caſt
hem i a pot, do Ꝓto clene broth, ſeeþ hem þ̄ᵗ þey be
tendre. take brede and þ̇ ſelf broth and drawe it up
yferʳ, take ſtrong Powdõ and Safroñ and Salt and caſt
þ to. take ayreñ and ſeeþ hem harde. take out the
zolk̓ and hewe the whyte þiñne, take the Pot fro þ̄ᵉ
fyre and caſt the whyte þiñne. meſſe the diſh̓ þwith
and lay the zolkes hool and flõ it with clow̓.

ᵖ Egurdouce. The term expreſſès *piccante dolce*, a mixture of
ſour and ſweet; but there is nothing of the former in the compoſi-
tion.   Vide Gloſſ.

۹ Concys ſeems to be a kind of known ſauce. V. Gloſſ.

ʳ y fere. Together.

Hares

Hares [s] in Talbotes [t]. XXIII.

Take Hares and hewe hem to gobettꝰ and seeþ hē wᵗ þe blode unwaisshed in broth. and whan þey buth y nouh: cast hem in colde wat̄. pyke and waisshe hē clene. cole [u] the broth and drawe it thurgh a stynoᷣ. take oþꝰ blode and cast in boylyng wat̄ seeþ it and drawe it thurgh a stynoᷣ. take Almānꝰ unblan̄ched. waisshe hem and grynde hem and temꝑ it up with the self broth. cast al in a pot. tak oynons and ꝑboile hē smyte hem small and cast hem in to þis Pot. cast þꝰinne Powdoᷣ fort. vyneg̃ ā salt.

Hares in Papdele [x]. XXIIII.

Take Hares ꝑboile hem in gode broth. cole the broth and waisshe the fleyssh. cast azeyn [y] to gydre. take obleys [z] oþꝰ wafrōus [a] in stede of lozeyns [b]. and cowche [c] in dysshes. take powdoᷣ douce and lay on salt the brōth and lay onowar̃d [d] ā messe forth.

[s] Haares, Contents. So again, N° 24.

[t] Talbotes. Mſ. Ed. N° 9, *Talbotays*.

[u] Cole. Cool. [x] Papdele. Qu. [y] azeyn. Again.

[z] obleys, called *oblatæ*; for which see Hearne ad Lib. Nig. I. p. 344. A kind of Wafer, otherwise called *Nebulæ*; and is the French *oublie*, *oble*. Leland, Collect. IV. p. 190. 327.

[a] wafrōns. Wafers. [b] loseyns. Vide Gloss.

[c] cowche. Lay.

[d] onoward. Upon it.

Connyng in Cynee ᶜ   XXV.

Take Coñyng and fmyte hem on peces. and feeþ
hem in gode broth. mynce Oynoñs and feeþ hē in
grece and in gode broth do þto. drawe a lyre of brede.
blode. vyneg and broth do þto with powdo fort.

Connyng in Grauey.   XXVI.

Take Cōnyng fmyte hem to pecys. pboile hem and
drawe hem with a gode broth with almand blanched
and brayed. do þinne fug and powdo gyng and boyle
it and the flefsh þwith. flo it w̃ fug ā w̃ powdo gyng
ā sūe forth.

Chykens in Gravey.   XXVII.

Take Chykens and sūe in the fame mañe and sūe
forth.

Fylett ᶠ of Galyntyne ᵍ.   XXVIII.

Take fylett of Pork and roft hem half ynowh fmyte
hem on pecys. drawe a lyo of brede and blode. and
broth and Vineg. and do þinne. feeþ it wele. and
do þinne powdo ā falt ā meffe it forth.

ᶜ Cynee. Vide Gloff.   ᶠ Fylettes. Fillets.
  ᵍ of Galyntyne. In Galyntyne. Cóntents, *rectius*. As for *Ga-*
lentine, fee the Gloff.

                                       Pygg

Pygg in ſawſe Sawge [h].   XXIX.

Take Pigg yſkaldid and quarꞇ hē and ſeeþ hem in
waꞇ and ſalꞇ, take hem and lat hem kele [i]. take pſel
ſawge. and grynde it with brede and zolkes of ayreñ
harde yſode. temp it up with vyneg ſū what thyk.
and lay the Pygg in a veſſell. and the ſewe onoward
and ſūe it forth.

Sawſe madame.   XXX.

Take ſawge. pſel. yſope. and ſaūay. ꝗnces. and
peer [h], garlek and Grapes. and fylle the gees þerwith.
and ſowe the hole þat no grece come out. and rooſt
hem wel. and kepe the grece þ̔ fallith þof. take galyntyne and grece and do in a poſſynet, whan the
gees buth roſted ynouh: take ā ſmyte hem on pecys.
and þat tat [l] is withinne and do it in a poſſynet and
put þinne wyne if it be to thyk. do þto powdo
of galyngale. powdo douce and ſalt and boyle the
ſawſe and dreſſe þ̔ Gees ī diſshes ā lay þ̔ ſowe onoward.

---

[h] Sawge. Sage. As ſeveral of them are to be uſed, theſe pigs
muſt have been ſmall.

[i] kele. Cool.

[k] Peares. Pears.

[l] that tat, i. e. that that. Vide Gloſſ.

Gees in hoggepot[m]. XXXI.

Take Gees and ſmyte hem on pecys. caſt hem in a Pot do þto half wyne and half wat̄. and do þto a gode qn̄tite of Oynons̄ and erbest. Set it oūe the fyre and coūe[n] it faſt. make a layō of brede and blode ā lay it þwith. do þto powdō fort and sūe it fort.

Carnel[o] of Pork. XXXII.

Take the brawn̄ of Swyne. ꝑboile it and grynde it ſmale and alay it up with zolkes of ayren. ſet it oūe[p] the fyre with white Grece and lat it not ſeeþ to faſt. do þinne Safron̄ ā powdō fort and meſſe it forth. and caſt þinne powdō douce. and sūe it forth.

Chykens̄[q] in Cawdel. XXXIII.

Take Chikens̄ and boile hem in gode broth and ramme[r] hem up. þenne take zolk of ayren ā þe broth and alye it togedre. do þto powdō of gyng and ſug ynowh ſafron̄ and ſalt. and ſet it oūe the fyre withoute boyllyng. and sūe the Chykēns hole[s] oþ ybroke and lay þe ſowe onoward.

m Hoggepot. Hodge-podge. *Ochepot*. Mſ. Ed. N° 22. French, *Hochepot*. Cotgrave. See Junii Etym. v. *Hotch-potch*.

n coūe. Cover. o Carnel, perhaps *Charnel*, from Fr. *Chaire*.

p oūe. Over. So again, N° 33.

q Chikens. Contents. So again in the next Recipe.

r ramme. Qu. preſs them cloſe together. s hole. Whole.

Chykens

Chᴊkens in hocchee ᵗ.　　xxxiiii.

Take Chykeñs and ſcald hem. take pſel and ſawge
withouͭe eny oꝯe erbes. take garlec ā grapꝯ and ſtoppe
the Chikeñs tul and ſeeþ hem in gode broth. ſo þat
þey may eſely be boyled þinne. meſſe hē ā caſt þto
powdꝰo dowce.

For to boile Feſāñt. Ptruch. Capons and Curlewꝯ.
　　　　　　　　　　　　　　　　xxxv.

Take gode broth and do þto the Fowle. and do
þto hool pepꝯ and flꝰo of canel a gode q̃ntite and lat
hem ſeeþ þwith. and meſſe it forth. and þ caſt þon
Podꝰo dowce.

Blank Mān̄g ᵘ.　　xxxvi.

Take Capoñs and ſeeþ hem, þenne take hem up.
take Almand blān̄ched. grynd hē and alay hē up with
the ſame broth. caſt the mylk in a pot. waiſshe rys
and do þto and lat it ſeeþ. þanne take brawn of Capoñs teere it ſmall and do þto. take white grece ſug̃
and ſalt and caſt þinne. lat it ſeeþ. þenne meſſe it

ᵗ Hochee. This does not at all anſwer to the French *Hachis*, or
our *Haſh*; therefore qu

ᵘ Blank Māng. Very different from ours. Vide Gloſſ.

D　　　　　　　　　　forth

forth and florifsh it with aneys in confyt rede op̉ whyt,
and with Almañd fryed in oyle, and sūe it forth.

Blank Defforre ˣ.   xxxvii.

Take Almand̉ blānched, gryndε hem and temp hem
up with whyte wyne, on fleifsh day with broth, and
caſt þinne floˊ of Rys. op̉ amydōn ʸ, and lye it þwith.
take brawñ' of Capoñs ygroñd. take fuḡ and falt and
caſt þto and florifsh it with aneys whyte. take a veffel
yholes ᶻ and put in fafroñ. and sūe it forth.

Morree ª.   xxxviii,

Take Almand̉ blānched, waifshe hem. grynde hem.
and temp hem up with rede wyne, and alye hem wᵗ
floˊ of Rys. do þto Pyñ yfryed. and coloˊ it with sāndr̉.
do þto powd̉o fort and powdŭ douce and falt. meffe it
forth and floˊ it ᵇ with aneys confyt whyte,

ˣ Blank Defforre. V. Gloff,

ʸ Amydōn. "Fine wheat flour fteeped in water, ſtrained and let
"ſtand to fettle, then drained and dried in the fun ; ufed for bread
" or in broths." Cotgrave. Ufed in Nº 68 for colouring white.

ᶻ yholes. Quære.

ª Morrce. Mˢ Ed 37. murrey. Ibid. II. 26. morrey; probably
from the mulberries ufed therein.

ᵇ floˊ it,⁻ Flourifh it.

Charlet [c].   XXXIX.

Take Pork and feeþ it wel. hewe it fmale. caſt it
in a panne. breke ayren̄ and do þto and ſwyng [d] it wel
togyder. do þto Cowe mylke and Safron̄ and boile it
togȳd. ſalt it & meſſe it forth.

Charlet yforced.   XX. II.

Take mylke and feeþ it, and ſwyng þwith zolkes of
Ayren̄ and do þto. and powdo̅ of gyng ſug̃. and Saf-
ron̄ and caſt þto. take the Charlet out of the broth
and meſſe it ī dyſshes, lay the ſewe onoward. flo̅ it
with powdo̅ douce. and ſūe it forth.

Cawdel ferry [e].   XX II. I.

Take flo̅ of Payndemayn [f] and gode wyne. and
drawe it togydre. do þto a grete q̄ntite of Sug̃ cypre.
or hony clarified. and do þto ſafron̄. boile it. and whan
it is boiled, alye it up with zolkes of ayren̄. and do
þto ſalt and meſſe it forth. and lay þon ſug̃ and powdo̅
gyng̃.

---

[c] Charlet; probably from the French, *chair*. Qu. Minced Meat,
and the next article, Forced Meat.

[d] ſwyng. Shake, mix.

[e] ferry. Quære. We have *Carpe in Ferry*, Lel. Coll. VI. p. 21.

[f] Payndemayn. White bread. Chaucer.

Juſshell.

Jusshell ᵍ.   XX
                          II. III.

Take brede ygrated and ayreñ and fwyng it togydre. do þto fafroñ, fawge. and falt. ₡ caſt brotħ.
þto. boile it & meſſe it forth.

Jusshell enforced ʰ.   XX
                          II. IIII.

Take and do þto as to charlet yforced. and sũe it
forth.

Mortrews ⁱ.   XX
                          II. V.

Take henñ and Pork and feeþ hem togȳd. take
the lyre of Henñ and of the Pork, and hewe it fmall
and gnde it all to douſt ᵏ. take brede ygted and do
þto, and temp it with the felf broth and alye it with
zolk of ayreñ, and caſt þon powdõ fort, boile it and

ᵍ Jusshell. See alfo next number. *Juſſell*, Mſ. Ed. 21, where
the Recipe is much the fame. Lat. *Juſcellum*, which occurs in the
old fcholiaſt on Juvenal iv. 23 ; and in Apicius, v. 3. Vide Du
Frefne, v. *Juſſellum* and *Juſcellum*, where the compofition confiſts
of *vinum*, *ova*, and *fagmen*, very different from this. Faber in
Thefauro cites *Juſcellum Gallinæ* from Theod. Prifcianus.

N. B. Nº XX. II. is omitted both here and in the Contents.

ʰ Jusshell enforced. As the *Charlet yforced* here referred to was
made of pork, compare Nº 40 with Nº 39. So in Theod. Prifcian
we have *Juſſellum Gallinæ*.

ⁱ Mortrews. Vide Gloſſ.

ᵏ douſt. Duſt, powder.

do þin powdo of gyng ſug. ſafron and ſalt. and loke
þ it be ſtondyng[1], and flo it with powdo gyng.

Mortrews blank. XX II. VI.

Take Pork and Henn and ſeeþ hem as to fore. bray
almand blanched, and temp hem up with the ſelf broth.
and alye the fleiſsh with the mylke and white flo of
Rys. and boile it. & do þin powdo of gyng ſugar and
look þat it be ſtondyng.

Brewet of Almony [m]. XX II. VII.

Take Conyng or kidd and hewe hem ſmall on
moſcels [n] oþ on pecys. þboile hem w the ſame broth,
drawe an almande mylke and do the fleiſsh þwith, caſt
þto powdo galyngale & of gyng with flo of Rys. and
colo it wiþ alkenet. boile it, ſait it. & meſſe it forth
with ſug and powdo douce.

l'eions [o] yſtewed. XX II. VIII.

Take peions and ſtop hem with garlec ypylled and
with gode erbes ihewe. and do hem in an erthen pot.

---

[1] ſtondyng. Stiff, thick.

[m] Almony. Almaine, or Germany. *Almany.* Fox, part I. p.
239. *Alamanie.* Chron. Sax. p. 242. V. ad Nº 71.

[n] moſcels. Morſels.

[o] Peiōns, Pejons, i. e. Pigeons. *j* is never written here in the
middle of a word.

caſt þto gode broth and whyte grece. Powdõ foſt.
ſafroñ vions & ſalt.

Loſeyns P.　　xx
II. IX.

Take gode broth and do ĩ an erthen pot, take flõ
of payndemayn and make þof paſt with waſ. and make
þof thynne foyles as pap ꝗ with a roller, drye it harde
and ſeeþ it ĩ broth take Cheſe ruayn ʳ grated and lay
it in diſsh with powdõ douce. and lay þon loſeyns
iſode as hoole as þou mizt ˢ. and above powdõ and
cheſe, and ſo twyſe or thryſe, & ſũe it forth.

Tarlett ᵗ.　　xx
II. X.

Take pork yſode and grynde it ſmall with ſafroñ,
medle it with ayreñ and raiſons of coraunce and powdõ fort and ſalt. and make a foile of dowhȝ ᵘ and
cloſe the fars ˣ þinne. caſt þ Tartlet ĩ a Panne with
faire waſ boillyng and ſalt, take of the clene Fleſsh
withoute ayreñ ⁊ boile it ĩ gode broth. caſt þto powdõ

ᴾ Loſeyns. Vide in Gloſſ.
ꝗ foyles as pap. *Leaves* of paſte as thin as *paper.*
ʳ Cheſe ruan. 166. Vide Gloſſ.
ˢ mizt. Might, i. e. can.
ᵗ Tarlettes. *Tartletes;* in the proceſs.
ᵘ foile of dowhz, or dowght. A leaf of paſte.
ˣ fars. Forced-meat.

douee

douce and falt, and meffe the tartlet ī difsh ⁊ helde ʏ
the fewe þonne.

Pynnonade ᶻ.
xx
II. XI.

Take Almand iblanched and drawe hem sūdell
thicke ᵃ with gode broth oþ with waᵗ and fet on the
fire and feeþ it, caſt þto zolk of ayreñ ydrawe. take
Pyn yfryed ī oyle oþer in grece and þto white Powdo
douce, fug and falt. ⁊ colo it wiþ alkenet a lytel.

Rofee ᵇ.
xx
II. XII.

Take thyk mylke as to fore welled ᶜ. caſt þto fug
a gode porciōn pyn. Dates ymynced. canel. ⁊ powdo
gyng and feeþ it, and alye it with flōs of white Rofis,
and flo of rys, cole it, falt it ⁊ meffe it forth. If
þ wilt in ſtede of Almañde mylke, take fwete crem
of kyne.

Cormarye ᵈ.
xx
II. XIII.

Take Colyandre ᵉ, Caraway fmale groñden, Powdo
of Pep and garlec ygroñde ī rede wyne, medle alle

ʏ helde. Caſt.

ᶻ Pynnonade. So named from the *Pynes* therein ufed.

ᵃ sūdell thicke. Somewhat thick, thickifh.

ᵇ Rofee. From the white rofes therein mentioned. See Nᵒ 41.
in Mf. Ed. but Nᵒ 47 there is totally different.

ᶜ welled, f. *wilted*; directed.

ᵈ Cormarye. Quære.   ᵉ Colyandre. Coriander.

þife

þiſe [f] togȳd and ſalt it, take loyn of Pork rawe and
fle of the ſkyn, and pryk it wel with a knyf and ſay
it in the ſawſe, rooſt þof what þ wilt, ⁊ kepe þ:t þ
fallith þfro ĩ the roſting and feeþ it in a poſſynet with
faire broth, ⁊ ſũe it forth witþ þ rooſt anoon [g].

Newe Noumbl of Deer.   II.XIIII.ˣˣ

Take noumbleş and waiſhe hem clene with waẽ
and ſalt and pboile hẽ ĩ waẽ. take hẽ up ā dyce hẽ.
do w hẽ as w ooþ noumbles.

Nota.   II.XV.ˣˣ

The Loyne of the Pork, is fro the hippe boon to
the hede.

Nota.   II.XVI.ˣˣ

The fylet buth two, that buth take oute of the
Peſtels [i].

Spynee [k].   II.XVII.ˣˣ

Take and make gode thik Almãnd mylke as tofore.
and do þin of flõ of hawthern [l]. and make it as a roſe.
⁊ ſũe it forth.

---

[f] þiſe. Theſe.   [g] anoon. Immediately.
[h] Peſtels. Legs.
[i] Spynee. As made of Haws, the berries of Spines, or Hawthorns.
[k] Hawthern. Hawthorn.

Chyryſe.

Chyryſe [1].

Take Almand unblanched, waiſshe hem, grynde hem, drawe hem up with gode broth. do þto thridde part of chiryſe. þ ſton. take oute and grynde hem ſmale, make a layo of gode brede ā powdo and ſalt and do þto. colo it with ſandr ſo that it may be ſtondyng, and floriſh it with aneys and with chewe-ryes, and ſtrawe þuppon and ſūe it forth.

Payn Fondew [m].

Take brede and frye it in grece oþ in oyle, take it and lay it in rede wyne. grynde it w̄ raiſoñs take hony and do it in a pot and caſt þinne gleyr [n] of ayreñ wiþ a litel wāt and bete it wele togider with a ſklyſe [o]. ſet it oūe the fir and boile it. and whan the hatte [p] ariſith to goon [q] oūe. take it adōn and kele it, and whan it is þ clariſiedr do it to the oþe with ſug and ſpices.

---

[1] Chyryſe. *Chiryſe* in the proceſs. *Cherriſeē.* Mſ. Ed. II. 18. *Chiryes* there are cherries. And this diſh is evidently made of Cherries, which probably were chiefly imported at this time from Flanders, though they have a Saxon name, cynȝe.

[m] fōndewe. Contents. It ſeems to mean *diſſolved.* V. *found* in Gloſſ.

[n] gleyres. Whites.   [o] Sklyſe. Slice.

[p] hatte. Seems to mean *bubling* or *ſwallop.*

[q] goon. Go.

     ſalt

falt it and loke it be ſtondyng, floriſh it with white
coliãdre in confyt.

Crotoñ ʳ.

Take the offal of Capoñs oꝑ of oꝑe bridd. make hē
clene and ꝑboile hem. take hem up and dyce hem.
take ſwete cowe mylke and caſt ꝑinne. and lat it boile.
take Payndemayn ˢ and of ꝑ ſelf mylke and drawe
thurgh a cloth and caſt it in a pot and lat it ſeeꝑ,
take ayren yſode. hewe the white and caſt ꝑto, and
alye the ſewe with zolkes of ayren rawe. coloo it with
ſafron. take the zolkes and fry hem and ſſoriſh hem
ꝑwith and with powdoo douce.

Vyne grace ᵗ.

Take ſmale ſyletꝓ of Pork and roſt hem half and
ſmyte hem to gobettꝓ and do hem in wyne ā Vyneꝶ
and Oynoñs ymyneed and ſtewe it yfere do ꝑto gode
powdos ā ſalt. ā ſuc it forth.

ʳ Crotōn. Mſ. Ed. 24. has *Craytōn*, but a different diſh.

ˢ Payndemayn. Whitebread. V. ad Nº 41.

ᵗ Vyne Grace. Named probably from *grees*, wild ſwine, and the
mode of dreſſing in *wine*. V. Gloſſ. voce *Vyne grace*.

Fonnell [u].

xx.
III. II.

Take Almand unblanched. grynde hem and drawe hem up with gode broth. take a lombe [x] or a kidde and half roſt hȳ. or the þridde [y] part, ſmyte hym i gobet and caſt hym to the mylke. take ſmale bridd yfaſted and yſtyned [z]. and do þto ſug, powdo of canell and ſalt, take zolkes of ayreñ harde yſode and cleene [a] a two and ypañced [b] with flo of canell and floriſh þ ſewe above. take alkenet fryed and yfoñdred [c] and droppe above with a feþ [d] and meſſe it forth.

Douce ame [e].

xx.
III. III.

Take gode Cowe mylke and do it in a pot. take pſel. ſawge. yſope. ſauñay and ooþ gode herbes. hewe hem and do hem in the mylke and ſeeþ hem. take capoñs half yroſted and ſmyte hem on pecys and do þto pyñ and hony clarified. ſalt it and colo it with ſafroñ ā ſue it forth.

---

[u] Fonnell. Nothing in the recipe leads to the etymon of this multifarious diſh.

[x] Lombe. Lamb.

[y] thridde. Third, per metatheſin.

[z] yfaſted and yſtyned.

[a] cleeue. cloven.

[b] ypāced. pounced.

[c] yfoñdred. melted, diſſolved.

[d] feþ'. feather.

[e] Douce Ame. *Quaſi*, a delicious diſh. V. Blank Deſire in Gloſſ. Titles of this tiſſue occur in Apicius. See Humelberg. p. 2.

Con-

Connyng in Cyrip [f].

xx.
III. IIII.

Take Cōnyng and feeþ hem wel ī good broth. take wyne greke and do þto with a porcion of vyneg and flo of canel, hoole clow quybibes hoole. and ooþ gode fpices with raifons coraunce and gyngyn ypared and ymynced. take up the conyng and fmyte hem on pecys and caft hem into the Siryppe and feeþ hem a litel on the fyr and sue it forth.

Leche Lumbard [g].

xx.
III. v.

Take rawe l'ork and pulle of the fkyn. and pyke out þ fkyn fynew and bray the Pork in a mort w ayren rawe do þto fug, falt, rayfons corance, dat mynced, and powdo of Peþ powdo gylofre. ā do it ī a bladder, and lat it feeþ til it be ynowhʒ. and whan it is ynowh, kerf it lefhe it [h] in likeneffe of a pefkodde [i], and take grete rayfons and grynde hem in a mort, drawe hem up wiþ rede wyne, do þto mylke of almand colo it with fanders ā fafron, and do þto powdo of peþ ā of

[f] Cyrip. In the procefs *Siryppe*. *Cirypp*, Contents. *Sirop*, or *Sirup*, as 133. *Syryp*, 132.

[g] Leche Lumbard. So called from the country. Randle Home fays, *Leach* is "a kind of jelly made of cream, ifing-glafs, fugar "and almonds, with other compounds."

[h] Lefhe it. Vide Gloff.

[i] Pefkodde. Hull or pod of a pea.

gilofre

gilofre and boile it. and whan it is iboiled: take powdo
of canel and gyng͞, and te̅p it up with wyne. and do
alle þife thyng togy̅d. and loke þat it be re̅nyns [k], and
lat it not feeþ aft that it is caſt togyder, a̅ ſue it
forth.

Connyng in clere broth. ^{XX,} III. VI.

Take Coñyng and ſmyte hem ĩ gobet and waifſh
hem and do hem in feyre wat and wyne, and feeþ
hem and ſkym hem. and whan þey buth iſode pyke
hem clene, and drawe the broth thurgh a fty̅no and
do the flefſh þwith ĩ a Poſſynet and ſtyne it [l]. and do
þto vyneg and powdo of gyng and a grete q̃ntite and
falt aft the laſt boillyng and ſue it forth.

Payn Ragoñ [m]. ^{XX,} III. VII.

Take hony fug   and clarifie it togydre. and boile
it with efy fy̅r, and kepe it wel fᵒ bre̅nyng and whan
it hath yboiled a while: take up a drope [n] þof wiþ þy
fyng and do it in a litel wat and loke if it hong [o] togyder. and take it fro the fyre and do þto the thrid-

---

[k] re̅nyns. Perhaps *thin*, from the old *renne*, to run. Vide Gloſſ.
[l] ſtyne it. Cloſe it. V. Gloſſ.
[m] Payn ragoñ. It is not at all explained in the Recipe.
[n] Drope. Drop.
[o] hong. Hing, or hang,

dendele ᴾ ā powdo̓ gyngen̊ and ſtere �126it togȳd til it bi-
gynne to thik and caſt it on a wcte ʳ table. leſh it
and sūe it forth ẘ fryed mete on fleſsh daẙ or on
fyſshe dayes.

Lete Lardes ˢ.   ˣˣ
III. VIII.

Take pſel and grynde with a Cowe mylk, medle it
with ayren̄ and lard ydyced take mylke aſt̄ þ̊ þ̊ haſt
to done ᵗ and myng ᵘ þwith. and make þ̊of dyūſe colours. If þ̊ wolt have zelow, do þ̊to ſafron̄ and no
pſel. If þ̊ wolt have it white: nonþ pſel ne ſafron̄
but do þ̊to amydon̄. If þ̊ wilt have rede do þ̊to ſandres. If þou wilt have pownas ˣ do þ̊to turneſole ʸ.
If þ̊ wilt have blak do þ̊to blode yſode and fryed. and
ſet on the fyr̄ ī as many veſſels as þ̊ haſt colours þerto

ᴾ thriddendele. Third part, perhaps, *of brede*, i. e. of bread,
may be caſually omitted here. V. Gloſſ.

�q ſtere. ſtir.   ʳ wete. wet.

ˢ Lete Lardes. *Lards* in form of Dice are noticed in the proceſs.
See Lel Coll. VI. p. 5. *Lete* is the Fr. *Lait*, milk. V. Nº 81.
or Brit. *Llaeth*. Hence, perhaps, *Lethe Cpyrus* and *Lethe Rube*.
Lel. Coll. IV. p. 227. But VI. p. 5, it is *Leche*.

ᵗ to done, i. e. done.

ᵘ myng. mix.

ˣ pownas. Qu.

ʸ turneſole. Not the flower *Heliotrope*, but a drug. Northumb.
Book, p. 3. 19. I ſuppoſe it to be *Turmeric*. V. Brooke's Nat.
Hiſt. of Vegetables, p. 9. where it is uſed both in victuals and for
dying.

and

and feeþ it wel and lay þife colours ī a cloth firſt ooﬆ
and fithen anoþ⁹ upon him. and fithen the þridde and
the ferthe. and p̄ﬀe it harde til it be all out clene.
And whan it is al colde, leﬁ it thynne, put it ī a
panne and fry it wel. and sūe it forth.

Furmente with Porpays [z].

Take Almand⁹ blanched. bray hem and drawe hem
up with faire waī, make furmente as before [a] and caﬆ
þ⁹ furmente þto.⁹ ꝼ meﬀe it with Porpays.

Perrey of Peſoñ [b].

Take peſoñ and feeþ hem faﬆ and cov̄e hem til þei
berﬆ. þenne take up hem and cole hem thurgh a
cloth. take oynoñs and mynce hē and feeþ hem in the
fame fewe and oile þwith,⁹ caﬆ þto⁹ fugur, falt and
fafroñ, and feeþ hem wel þaﬆī⁹ and sūe hem forth.

Peſoñ of Almayne [c].

Take white peſoñ, waiſshe hem feeþ hem a grete
while. take hem and cole hem thurgh a cloth, waiſshe

[z] Porpays. *Porpeys*, Contents, and fo Nᵒ 116. Porpus.
[a] as before. This is the firſt mention of it.
[b] Perrey of Peſoñ, i. e. Peas. *Perrey* feems to mean pulp;
vide Nᵒ 73. Mr. Ozell in Rabelais, IV. c. 6o. renders *Puree de
pois* by *Peas foup.*
[c] Almayne. Germany; called Almony Nᵒ 47.

hem

hem ĩ colde waͭ til the hulles go off, caſt hem in a
pot and coũe þ no breth ᵈ go out. and boile hem right
wel. and caſt þinne gode mylke of almand͛ and a ꝑtye
of flõ of Rys wiþ powdõ gyng͛ ſafroñ, and ſalt.

Chych ᵉ.   xx.
iii. xii.

Take chich͛ and wry hem ᶠ ĩ aſhès all nyʒt, oþ lay
hem in hoot aymers ᵍ, at morrowe ʰ, waiſhe hem in
clene waͭ and do hem oũe the fire with clene waͭ.
ſeeþ hẽ up and do þto oyle, garlec, hole ſafroñ. powdõ
fort and ſalt, ſeeþ it and meſſe it forth.

Frenche ⁱ.   xx.
iii. xiii.

Take and ſeeþ white peſon and take oute þ perrey ᵏ
ꝗ þboile erbis ꝗ hewe hẽ grete ꝗ caſt hẽ ĩ a pot w the
perrey pulle oynoñs ꝗ ſeeþ hẽ hole wel ĩ waͭ ꝗ do hẽ
to þ Perrey w oile ꝗ ſalt, colõ it w ſafroñ ꝗ meſſe it
and caſt þon powdõ douce.

ᵈ breth. Breath, air, ſteam. MſΤ. Ed. N° 2.
ᵉ Chyches. *Viciæ*, vetches. In Fr. *Chiches*.
ᶠ wry hem. *Dry hem*, or *cover hem*. Chaucer, v: wrey.
ᵍ Aymers. Embers; of which it is evidently a corruption.
ʰ at morrowe. Next Morning.
ⁱ Frenche. Contents have it more fully, *Frenche Owtes*. V. ad
N° 6.
    ᵏ Perrey. Pulp. V. ad Nⁿ 70.

Makke[1].   xx.
iii. xiiii.

Take drawen benes and seeþ hē wel. take hē up of the waᵗ and caſt hē in a morᵗ grynde hem al to douſt til þei be white as eny mylk, chawf[m] a litell rede wyne, caſt þamong in þ gryndyng, do þto ſalt, leſhe it ī diſsh. þanne take Oynoñs and mynce hem ſmale and ſeeþ hem ī oile til þey be al broñ[n]. and floriſsh the diſsh þwith. and sūe it forth.

Aquapatys[o].   xx.
iii. xv.

Pill garlec and caſt it in a pot with waᵗ and oile. and ſeeþ it, do þto ſafroñ, ſalt, and powdo̅ forᵗ and dreſſe it forth hool.

Salat.   xx.
iii. xvi.

Take pſel, ſawge, garlec, chiboll, oynoñs, leek, borage, mynt, porrect[p], fenel and ton treſſis[q], rew, roſemarye, purſlarye[r], laue and waiſche hem clene,

---

[1] Makke. *Ignotum.*

[m] Chawf. Warm.

[n] broñ. Brown.

[o] Aquapatys. *Aquapates*, Contents. Perhaps named from the water uſed in it.

[p] Porrectes. Fr. *Porrette.*

[q] Ton treſſis. Creſſes. V. Gloſſ.

[r] Purſlarye. Purſlain.

F   pike

pike hem, pluk hē ſmall wiþ þyn ᵃ honde and myng
hem wel with rawe oile. lay on vyneg̃ and ſalt, and
ſūe it forth.

Fenkel in Soppes.   XX. III. XVII.

Take blades of Fenkel. ſhrede hem not to ſmale,
do hem to ſeeþ in wat̄ and oile and oynoñs mynced
þwith. do þto ſafroñ and ſalt and powdo̅. douce. ſūe
it forth. take brede ytoſted and lay the ſewe onoward.

Clat ᵗ.   XX. III. XVIII.

Take elena campana and ſeeþ it wat̄ ᵘ. take it up
and grynde it wel in a morf̄. temp it up w̄ ᵗ ayreñ
ſafroñ and ſalt and do it ou̅ the fire and lat it not
boile. caſt above powdo̅ douce and ſūe it forth.

Appulmoy ˣ.   XX. III. XIX.

Take Apples and ſeeþ hem in wat̄, drawe hem
thurgh a ſtÿno̅. take almañde mylke ⁊ hony and flo̅
of Rys, ſafroñ and powdo̅ fort and ſalt. and ſeeþ it
ſtondyng ʸ.

ᵃ þyn. thine.   ᵗ Clar. Qu.
ᵘ water ; r. *in water*, as in Nº 79.
ˣ Appulmoy. *Appulmos.* Mſ. Ed. Nº 17. named from the apples
employed. V. Nº 149.
ʸ ſtondyng. thick.

Slete

Slete ᶻ Soppes.

xx.
IIII.

Take white of Lek⁹ and flyt hem, and do hem to
feeþ ī wyne, oile and falt, roft brede and lay in
dyfsh⁹ and the fewe above and sūe it forth.

Letelorye ª.

xx.
IIII. I.

Take Ayrēn and wryng hem thurgh a ftȳnó and
do þto cowe mylke with butt and fafroñ and falt and
feeþ it wel. lefhe it. and loke þat it be ftondyng. and
sūe it forth.

Sowp⁹ Dorry ᵇ.

xx.
IIII. II.

Take Almānd⁹ brayed, drawe hem up with wyne.
boile it, caft þuppon fafroñ and falt, take brede itofted
in wyne. lay þof a leyne ᶜ and anoþ⁹ of þ fewe and
alle togydre. florifh it with fug⁹ powdó gyng⁹ and sūe
it forth.

Rape ᵈ.

xx.
IIII. III.

Take half fyg⁹ and half raifoñs pike hem and waifshe
hem in wat fkalde hem in wyne. bray hem in a mort,

ᶻ Slete. flit.

ª Letelorye. The latter part of the compound is unknown, the
firft is Fr. *Lait,* milk. Vide Nº 68.

ᵇ Sowpes Dorry. Sops endorfed. V. *Dorry* in Gloff.

ᶜ A leyne. a layer.

ᵈ Rape. A diffyllable, as appears from *Rapey* in the Contents.
Rapy, Mf. Ed. Nº 49. *Rapee,* ibid. II. 28.

and

and drawe hem thurgh a ſtrayñõ. caſt hem in a pot
and þwiþ powdõ of pep and ooþ good powdõs. alay
it up with ſlõ of Rys. and colõ it with ſandres. ſalt
it: ꝗ meſſe it forth.

Sawſe Sarzyne ^e.   xx.
   IIII.IIII.

Take hepp and make hem clene. take Almãnd
blañched. frye hem ĩ oile and bray hem in a morꝉ
with hepp. drawe it up with rede wyne, and do þin
ſug̃ ynowhȝ with Powdõ fort. lat it be ſtondyng, and
alay it with ſlõ of Rys. and colõ it with alkenet and
meſſe it forth. and floriſh it with Põme garnet. If þ
wilt in fleſſhe day ſeeþ Capoñs and take the brawñ
and teſe hem ſmal and do þto. and make the lico ^f of
þis broth.

Creme of Almãnd.   xx.
   IIII.v.

Take Almãnd blañched, grynde hem and drawe
hem up thykke, ſet hem oũe the fyre ꝗ boile hem.
ſet hem adoũ and ſpryng ^g hem with Vyneg̃, caſt hem
abrode uppon a cloth and caſt uppon hem ſug̃. whan
it is colde gadre it togydre and leſhe it in dyſſh.

<hr>

^e Sawſe Sarzyne. *Sauſe.* Contents. *Saracen,* we preſume, from
the nation or people. There is a Recipe in Mſ. Ed. Nº 54 for a
Bruet of *Sarcyneſſe,* but there are no pomgranates concerned.

^f lico. liquor.   ^g ſpryng. ſprinkle.

Grewel

Grewel of Almand.   xx. iiii. vi.

Take Almand blanched. bray hē w̄ᵗ oot meel ʰ. and draw hē up with waī. caſt þon Safroñ ⁊ ſalt ⁊c.

Cawdel of Almand mylk.   xx. iiii. vii.

Take Almand blanched and drawe hem up with wyne, do þto powdō of gyng and ſug and colō it with Safroñ. boile it and ſūe it forth.

Jowt of Almand Mylké.   xx. iiii. viii.

Take erbes, boile hem, hewe hem and grynde hem ſmale. and drawe hem up with waī. ſet hem on the fire and ſeeþ the rowt with the mylke. and caſt þon ſug ⁊ ſalt. ⁊ ſūe it forth.

Fygey ᵏ.   xx. iiii. ix.

Take Almand blanched, grynde hem and drawe hem up with waī and wyne: quarī fyg hole raiſoñs. caſt þto powdō gyng and hony clarified. ſeeþ it wel ⁊ ſalt it, and ſūe forth.

ʰ oot meel. oat-meal.

ⁱ Jowtes. V. ad N° 60.

ᵏ Fygey. So named from the figs therein uſed. A different Recipe, Mſ. Ed. N° 3, has no figs.

Pochee.

Pochee [1].

Take Ayren̄ and breke hem ĭ fcaldyng hoot waŧ. and whan þei bene fode ynowh. take hē up and take zolkes of ayren and rawe mylke and fwyng hem to-gydre, and do þto powdō gyng̃ fafron̄ and falt, fet it oūe the fire, and lat it not boile, and take ayren̄ ifode ꝼ caſt þ̄ few onoward. ꝼ sūe it forth.

Brewet of Ayrēn.

Take ayren̄, waŧ and butŧ, and feeþ hem yfere with fafron̄ and gobett of chefe. wryng ayren̄ thurgh a ſtraynō. whan the waŧ hath foden awhile; take þēne the ayren̄ and fwyng hē with vious. and caſt þto. fet it oūe the fire and lat it not boile. and sūe it forth.

Macrows [m].

Take and make a thynne foyle of dowh. and kerve it on peces, and caſt hem on boillyng waŧ ꝼ feeþ it wele. take chefe and grate it and butŧ caſt bynethen and above as lofyns. and sūe forth.

---

[1] Pochee. Poached eggs. Very different from the prefent way.

[m] Macrows. *Maccherone*, according to the Recipe in *Altieri*, cor-refponds nearly enough with our procefs; fo that this title feems to want mending, and yet I know not how to do it to fatisfaction.

Toſtee.

Toſtee [n]. XX. IIII. XIII.

Take wyne and hony and foñd it [o] togȳd and ſkym it clene. and feeþ it long, do þto powdō of gynḡ. peꝑ and ſalt, toſt brede and lay the few þto. kerue pecys of gynḡ and flō it þwith and meſſe it forth.

Gyngawdry [p]. XX. IIII. XIIII.

Take the Powche [q] and the Lyuō [r] of haddok, cod-lyng and hake [s] and of ooþ fiſshe, ꝑboile hē, take hē and dyce hem ſmall, take of the ſelf broth and wyne, a layō of brede of galyntyne with gode powdōs and ſalt, caſt þat fyſshe þinne and boile it. ⁊ do þto amy-doñ. ⁊ colō it grene.

Erbowle [t]. XX. IIII. XV.

Take bolas and ſcald hem with wyne and drawe hem with [u] a ſtȳnō do hem in a pot, clarify hony and do þto with powdō fort. and flō of Rys. Salt it ⁊ floriſh it w̌ whyte aneys. ⁊ sꝰe it forth.

---

[n] Toſtee. So called from the toaſted bread.

[o] fōnd it. mix it. [p] Gyngawdry. Qu.

[q] Powche. Crop or ſtomach.

[r] Lyuō. Liver. V. N° 137.

[s] Hake. "Aſellus alter, ſive Merlucius, Aldrov." So Mr. Ray. See Pennant, III. p. 156.

[t] Erbowle. Perhaps from the *Balas*, or Bullace employed.

[u] with, i. e. thurgh or thorough.

Reſmolle.

Refmolle ˣ.　　　　　ᶜᶜ. IIII. XVI.

Take Almãnd blãnched and drawe hem up with
waꝛ̃ and alye it with flõ of Rys and do ꝑto powdõ of
gyng̃ fug̃ and falt, and loke it be not ſtõndyng ʸ,
meſſe it and ſũe it forth.

Vyãnde Cypre ᶻ.　　　　　ᶜᶜ. IIII. XVII.

Take oot mele and pike out the ſtõn and grynde
hem fmale, and drawe hem thurgh a ſtŷnõ. take mede
oꝥ wyne ifonded in fug̃ and do ꝥiſe ꝥinne. do ꝑto
powdõ and falt, and alay it with flõ of Rys and do
ꝥat it be ſtondyng. if thou wilt on fleſh day: take
henñ and pork yfode ⁊ grynde hem fmale and do ꝑto.
⁊ meſſe it forth.

Vyande Cypre of Samõn ᵃ.　　　　ᶜᶜ. IIII. XVIII.

Take Almãnd and bray hem unblãnched. take cal-

ˣ Refmølle. From the Rice there ufed; for Mſ. Ed. II. Nᵒ 5.
has *Ryſmoyk*, where *moy'e* feems to be Fr. *molle*, as written alfo in the
Roll. *Rice molens potage.* Lel. Coll. VI. p. 26.

ʸ Not ſtondyng. Thin, diluted. V. Nᵒ 98. Not to [too] ſtondyng, 121.

ᶻ Cypre. *Cipre*, Contents here and Nᵒ 98.

ᵃ Samõn. Salmon.

war

war [b] Samon and feeþ it in lewe wat [c] drawe up þyn almand with the broth. pyke out the bon out of the fyfsh clene ⁊ grynde it fmall ⁊ caft þy mylk ⁊ þ togyd ⁊ alye it w flo of Rys, do þto powdo fort, fug ⁊ falt ⁊ colo it w alkenet ⁊ loke þ hit be not ftondyng and meffe it forth.

Vyannd Ryal.

xx.
iiii. xix.

Take wyne greke, oþ rynyfshe wyne and hony clarified þwith. take flo of rys powdo of Gyng oþ of pep ⁊ canel. oþ flo of canel. powdo of clow. fafron. fug cypre. mylberyes, oþ fandr. ⁊ medle alle þife togid. boile it and falt it. and loke þat it be ftondyng.

Compoft [d].

c.

Take rote of pfel. pafternak of rafens [e]. fcrape hem and waifthe hē clene. take rap ⁊ caboch ypared and

---

[b] calwar. Salwar, Nº 167. R. Holme fays, "*Calver* is a term "ufed to a Flounder when to be boiled in oil, vinegar, and fpices "and to be kept in it." But in Lancafhire Salmon newly taken and immediately dreffed is called *Calver Salmon*: and in Littleton *Salar* is a young falmon.

[c] lewe water. warm. V. Gloff.

[d] Compoft. A compofition to be always ready at hand. Holme, III. p. 78. Lel. Coll. VI. p. 5.

[e] Pafternak of rafēns. Qu.

G

icorne.

icorne f. take an erthen pāne w̃ clene waꝑ ꝫ ſet it on
the fire. caſt all þiſe ꝑinne. whan þey buth boiled caſt
ꝑto peeꝛ ꝫ ꝑboile hem wel. take þiſe thyng up ꝫ lat
it kele on a fair cloth, do ꝑto ſalt whan it is colde in
a veſſel take vineg̃ ꝫ powd̃o ꝫ ſafron̄ ꝫ do ꝑto. ꝫ lat
alle þiſe thing lye þin al nyzt oꝑ al day, take wyne
greke and hony clarified togid̃ lumbarde muſtard ꝫ
raiſon̄s corance al hool. ꝫ grynde powd̃o of canel
powd̃o douce ꝫ aneys hole. ꝫ fenell ſeed. take alle
þiſe thyng ꝫ caſt togȳd ī a pot of erthe. and take þof
whan þ wilt ꝫ sūe forth.

Gele ᵍ of Fyſh.   c. i.

Take Tench, pykes ʰ, eelys, turbut and plays ⁱ,
kerue hē to pecys. ſcalde hē ꝫ waiſche hē clene. drye

---

f ypared and icorne. The firſt relates to the Rapes, the ſecond
to the Caboches, and means carved or cut in pieces.

g Gele. Jelly. Gelee, Contents here and in the next Recipe.
Gely, Mſ. Ed. Nº 55, which preſents us with much the ſame pre-
ſcription.

h It is commonly thought this fiſh was not extant in England till
the reign of H. VIII.; but ſee Nº 107. 109. 114. So Lucys, or
Tenchis, Mſ. Ed. II 1. 3. Pygus or Tenchis, II. 2. Pikys, 33.
Chaucer, v. Luce; and Lel. Coll. IV. p. 226. VI. p. 1. 5. Luce
ſalt. Ibid. p. 6. Mr. Topham's Mſ. written about 1250, mentions
Lupos aquaticos ſive Luceos amorgſt the fiſh which the fiſhmonger
was to have in his ſhop. They were the arms of the Lucy family
ſo early as Edw. I. See alſo Pennant's Zool. III. p. 280, 4to.

i Plays. Plaiſe, the fiſh.

hē

hẽ ẘ a cloth do hẽ ĩ a pāne do p̓to half vyneg̓ ⅋ half
wyne ⅋ feeþ it wel. ⅋ take the Fyfshe and pike it
clene, cole the broth thurgh a cloth ĩto an erthen
pāne. do p̓to powdo̓ of pep and fafroñ ynowh. lat it
feeþ and fkym it wel whan it is yfode.̓ dof ᵏ þ grees
clene, cowche fifshe on chargeo̓s ⅋ cole the fewe tho-
row a cloth onoward ⅋ fũe it forth.

Gele of Flefsh. .c. ii.

Take fwyñ feet ⅋ fnowt̓ and the eerys ¹. capons.
cōnyng̓ calu̓ fete. ⅋ waifche hẽ clene. ⅋ do hẽ to feeþ
in the þriddel ᵐ of wyne ⅋ vyneg̓ and wat̄ and make
forth as bifore.

Chyfanne ⁿ. .c. iii.

Take Roches. hole Tench̓ and plays ⅋ fmyte hem
to gobett̓. fry hẽ ĩ oyle blānche almānd. fry hẽ ⅋ caft
p̓to raifoñs corance make lyo̓ of cruft of brede of rede
wyne ⅋ of vyneg̓ þ þridde part þw fyg̓ drawen ⅋ do
p̓to powdo̓ fort and falt. boile it. lay the Fifshe ĩ an
erthen panne caft the fewe p̓to. feeþ oynoñs ymy̓nced
⅋ caft p̓ine. kepe hit and ete it colde.

ᵏ Dof, i. e. do of.
¹ Eerys. Ears.
ᵐ Thriddel. V. ad Nº 67.
ⁿ Chyfanne. Qu.

Congur

Congur ° in Sawſe. .c. iiii.

Take the Cong and ſcald hȳ. and ſmyte hȳ in
pecys ⁊ ſeeþ hym. take pſel. mynt. pelet. roſmarye. ⁊
a litul ſawge. brede and ſalt, powdo fort and a litel
garlec, clow a lite, take and grynd it wel, drawe it
up with vyneg þurgh a cloth. caſt the fyſsh ī a veſſel
and do þ ſewe onoward ⁊ ſue it forth.

Rygh ᴾ in Sawſe. .c. v.

Take Ryghzes and make hem clene and do hē to
ſeeþ. pyke hē clene and frye hem ī oile. take Almānd
and grynde hē ī waʈ or wyne, do þto almand blānched
hole fryed ī oile. ⁊ corāce ſeeþ the lyoʒ grynde it
ſmale ⁊ do þto garlec ygronde ⁊ litel ſalt ⁊ vions
powdo fort ⁊ ſafron ⁊ boile it yfere, lay the Fyſshe
in a veſſel and caſt the ſewe þto. and meſſe it forth
colde.

Makerel in Sawſe. .c. vi.

Take Makerels and ſmyte hem on pecys. caſt hem
on waʈ and vions. ſeeþ hem with mynt and wiþ ooþ
erbes, colo it grene or zelow, and meſſe it forth.

° Congur. The Eel called *Congre*. *Sawce*, Contents here, and
Nº 105, 106.

ᴾ Rygh. A Fiſh, and probably the *Ruffe*.

Pykes in braſey [q]. .c. VII.

Take Pykes and undo hem on þͤ wombꝰ [r] and waiſshe hem clene and lay hem on a rooſt Irne [s] þenne take gode wyne and powdoᷣ gyngꝰ ⁊ ſugꝰ good wone [t] ⁊ ſalt, and boile it ĩ an erthen panne ⁊ meſſe forth þͤ pyke ⁊ lay the ſewe onoward.

Porpeys in broth. .c. VIII.

Make as þou madeſt Noumbles of Fleſh with oynoñs.

Balloc [u] broth. .c. IX.

Take Eelys and hilde [x] hem and kerue hem to pecys and do hem to ſeeþ in wat̃ and wyne ſo þat it be a litel ouꝰ ſtepid [y]. do þꝰto ſawge and ooþꝰ erbis wͭ few [z] oynoñs ymynced, whan the Eelis buth ſoden ynowȝ do hem in a veſſel, take a pyke and kerue it to gobettꝰ and ſeeþ hym in the ſame broth do þꝰto powdoᷣ gyngᷣ galyngale canel and pep̃, ſalt it and caſt the Eelys þꝰto ⁊ meſſe it forth.

[q] Braſey. Qu.
[r] Wombs. bellies.
[s] rooſt Irene. a roaſting iron.
[t] good wone. a good deal. V. Gloſſ.
[u] Balloc. *Ballok*, Contents.
[x] hilde. ſkin.
[y] on ſtepid. ſteeped therein. V. N° 110.
[z] few, i. e. a few.

Eles

Eles in. Brewet. .c. x.

Take Cruſt of brede and wyne and make a lyõ, do þto oynoñs ymynced, powdõ. ⁊ canel. ⁊ a litel waɼ and wyne. loke þat it be ſtepid, do þto ſalt, kerue þin Eelis ⁊ ſeeþ hē wel and ſūe hem forth.

Cawdel of Samõn. .c.xi.

Take the gutt of Samõn and make hem clene. pboile hem a lytell. take hem up and dyce hem. ſlyt the white of Lekes and kerue hem ſmale. cole the broth and do the lek þinne w oile and lat it boile togyd yfere ᵃ. do the Samõn icorne þin, make a lyõ of Almãnd mylke ⁊ of brede ⁊ caſt þto ſpices, ſafroñ and ſalt, ſeeþ it wel. and loke þat it be not ſtondyng.

Plays in Cyce. .c. xii.

Take Plays and ſmyte hem ᵇ to pecys and fry hem in oyle. drawe a lyõ of brede ⁊ gode broth ⁊ vynēg. and do þto powdõ gyng. canel. pep and ſalt and loke þ it be not ſtondyng.

For to make Flaumpeyns. .c. xiii.

Take clene pork and boile it tendre. þenne hewe it ſmall and bray it ſmal in a morɼ. take fyg and boile

---

ᵃ togyd yfere. One of theſe ſhould be ſtruck out.
ᵇ Vide Nᵒ 104. Qu.

hem

hem tendre in ſmale ale. and bray hem and tendre
cheſe þwith. þēne waiſthe hem ī waꞇ ⁊ þene lẏ ᶜ hem
alle togid w̄ Ayreñ, þenne take powdõ of pep. or els
powdõ marchãnt ⁊ ayreñ and a porciõn of ſafroñ and
ſalt. þeñe take blank ſug̃: eyreñ ⁊ flõ ⁊ make a paſt
w̄ a roller, þene make þof ſmale pelett ᵈ. ⁊ fry hē broū
ī clene grece ⁊ ſet hem aſyde. þenne make of þ ooþ
deel ᵉ of þ paſt long coffyns ᶠ ⁊ do þ comade ᵍ þin. and
cloſe hē faire with a coūʐõ ʰ, ⁊ pynche hē ſmale about.
þāne kyt aboue foure oþ ſex wayes, þanne take eūy ⁱ
of þ kuttyng up, ⁊ þene colõ it w̄ zolkes of Ayreñ,
and plãnt hem thick, īto the flaumpeyns above þ þ
kutteſt hē ⁊ ſet hē ī an ovene and lat hem bake eſelich ᵏ.
and þanne ſūe hem forth.

For to make Noumbl̃ in Lent.   .c. XIIII.

Take the blode of pykes oþ of cong̃ and nyme ˡ the
pañch of pykes. of cong̃ and of grete code lyng ᵐ, ⁊

ᶜ lẏ. mix.
ᵈ Pelettes. *Pelotys*, Mſ. Ed. Nᵒ 16. Balls, pellets, from Fr. *pelote*.
ᵉ deel. deal, i. e. part, half.
ᶠ Coffyns. Pies without lids.
ᵍ comade. Qu.
ʰ coūʐõ. coverture, a lid.   ⁱ eūy. every.
ᵏ eſelich. eaſily, gently.
ˡ nyme. take. Perpetually uſed in Mſ. Ed. from Sax. nɪman.
ᵐ code lyng. If a Codling be a *ſmall cod*, as we now underſtand
it, *great codling* ſeems a contradiction in terms.

4   boile

boile hē tendre ⁊ mynce hē fmale ⁊ do hē ī þat blode.
take cruſt of white brede ⁊ ſtȳne it thurgh a cloth.
þenne take oynoñs iboiled and mynced. take pep and
ſafroñ. wyne. vyneg ayſell ⁿ oþ aleg ⁊ do þto ⁊ sūe
forth.

For to make Chawdon ° for Lent.   .c. xv.

Take blode of gurnard and cong ⁊ þ pānch of gurnard and boile hē tendre ⁊ mynce hē fmale, and make
a lyre of white Cruſt and oynoñs ymynced, bray it ī
a morᵗ ⁊ þanne boile it togyd til it be ſtondyng. þenne
take vyneg oþ ayſell ⁊ ſafroñ ⁊ put it þto and sūe it
forth.

Furmente with Porpeys.   .c. xvi.

Take clene whete and bete it fmall in a morᵗ and
fanne out clene the douſt, þenne waiſthe it clene and
boile it tyl it be tendre and broū. þanne take the
fecunde mylk of Almānd ⁊ do þto. boile hē togid til
it be ſtondyng, and take þ firſt mylke ⁊ alye it up
wiþ a peñe ᴾ. take up the porpays out of the Furmente ⁊ leſhe hem ī a diſhe with hoot waᵗ. ⁊ do ſafroñ

ᴬ Ayſell. Eifel, vinegar. Littleton.
● Chawdōn. V. Gloſſ.
ᴾ Penne. Feather, or pin. Mſ. Ed. 28.

to þ furmente. and if the porpays be falt. feeþ it by
hȳ felf, and fūe it forth.

Fylett in galyntyne. .c. xvii.

Take Pork, and roft it tyl the blode be tryed out ȝ
þ broth ꝗ. take cruſt of brede and bray hem ī a morꝉ, ā
drawe. hē thurgh a cloth with þ broth, þenne take oynoñs ā leſhe hem on brede ā do to the broth. þanne take
pork, and leſhe it clene with a dreſſyng knyf and caſt
it into þ pot broth, ȝ lat it boile til it be more tendre.
þanne take þat lyō þto. þāne take a porciō of pep
and fañdr ȝ do þto. þanne take pſel ȝ yſope ȝ mynce
it ſmale ȝ do þto. þāne take rede wyne oþ white grece
ȝ rayſoñs ȝ·do þto. ȝ lat it boile a lytel.

Veel in buknade ͬ. .c. xviii.

Take fayr Veel and kyt it in ſmale pecys and boile
it tendre ī fyne broth oþ in waꝉ. þanne take white
brede oþ waſtel ͥ, and drawe þof a white .... lyō
wiþ fyne broth, and do þ lyō to the Veel, ȝ do ſafroñ
þto, þāne take pſel ȝ bray it ī a morꝉ ȝ the Juys ͭ
þof do þto, and þāne is þis half zelow ȝ half grene.

ꝗ the broth. Suppoſed to be prepared beforehand.
ͬ Buknade. V. N° 17.
ͥ Waſtel. V. Gloſſ.
ͭ Juys. Juice.

H   þāne

þāne take a porciōn of wyne ⁊ powdõ marchant ⁊ do
þto and lat it boile wele, and do þto a litel of ᵘ vyneg̃.
⁊ sũe forth.

Sooles in Cynee ˣ.   .C. XIX.

Take Sooles and hylde hem, feeþ hem in waᵢ̄,
fmyte hē on pecys and take away the fyũnes. take
oynoñs iboiled ⁊ grynde the fynn þw and brede.
drawe it up with the felf broth. do þto powdõ fort,
fafroñ ⁊ hony clarified with falt, feeþ it alle yfere.
broile the fooles ⁊ meffe it ī dyfsh ⁊ lay the fewe
above. ⁊ sũe forth.

Tench in Cynee.   XX. VI.

Take Tench and fmyte hem to pecys, fry hem,
drawe a lyõ of Rayfoñs corañce witþ wyne and waᵢ̄,
do þto hool raifoñs ⁊ powdõ of gyng̃ of clowes of
canel of peþ do the Tench þto ⁊ feeþ hē w̃ fug̃ cypre
⁊ falt. ⁊ meffe forth.

ᵘ litel of vyneg̃. We fay, *a little vinegar*, omitting *ef*. So 152,
a l.tull of lard.

ˣ Cynee. *Cyney*, Contents, both here and Nᵈ 120. 123. See
before, N° 25.

Oyfters

Oyſters in Gravey. XX VI. I.

Schyl [y] Oyſters and ſeeþ hem in wyne and in hare [z] own broth. cole the broth thurgh a cloth. take almand blan̄ched, grynde hē and drawe hē up with the ſelf broth. & alye it wiþ flo of Rys. and do the oyſters þinne, caſt in powdo of gyng, ſug, macys. ſeeþ it not to ſtondyn̄g and ſue forth.

Muſkels [a] in brewet. XX. VI. II.

Take muſkels, pyke hem, ſeeþ hem with the owne broth, make a lyo of crust [b] & vyneg do in oynon̄s mynced. & caſt the muskels þto & ſeeþ it. & do þto powdo wt a lytel ſalt & ſafron the ſamewiſe make of oyſters.

Oyſters in Cynee. XX. VI. III.

Take Oyſters ꝑboile hem ī her owne broth, make a lyo of crust of brede & drawe it up wiþ the broth and vyneg mynce oynon̄s & do þto with erbes. & caſt the oyſters þinne. boile it. & do þto powdo fort & ſalt. & meſſe it forth.

[y] Schyl. ſhell, take of the ſhells.

[z] hare. their. *her.* N° 123. Chaucer.

[a] Muſkles. *muſkels* below, and the Contents. Muſcles.

[b] cruſtes, i. e. of bread.

Cawdel of Muſkels.   xx.
vi. iiii.

Take and feeþ muſkels, pyke hem clene, and waiſshe
hem clene ī wyne. taᵇe almand ⁊ bray hē. take sōme
of the muſkels and grynde hē. ⁊ ſome hewe ſmale,
drawe the muſkels ygrōnd w the ſelf broth. wryng
the almānd with faire waᵗ. do alle þiſe togiđ. do þto
vious and vyneg. take whyte of lek ⁊ þboile hē
wel. wryng oute the waᵗ and hewe hē ſmale. caſt
oile þto w oynons þboiled ⁊ mynced ſmale do þto
powdo fort, ſafron and ſalt. a lytel feeþ it not to to ᵉ
ſtondyng ⁊ meſſe it forth.

Mortrews of Fyſsh.   xx.
vi. v.

Take codlyng, haddok, oþ hake and lynos with
the rawnes ᵈ and ſeeþ it wel in waᵗ. pyke out þ
bones, grynde ſmale the Fyſshe, drawe a lyo of almānd ⁊ brede w the ſelf broth, and do the Fyſshe
gronden þto. and feeþ it and do þto powdo fort, ſaf-
rōn and ſalt, and make it ſtondyng.

Laumpreys in galyntyne.   xx.
vi. vi.

Take Laumpreys and fle ᵉ hem with vyneg oþ with
white wyne ⁊ ſalt, ſcalde hē ī waᵗ. ſlyt hem a litel

ᶜ to to, i. e. too too. Vide Nº 17.
ᵈ rawnes. roes.   ᵉ fle. flay, kill.

at

at þ nauel. . . . . . . ⁊ reſt a litel at the nauel. take out the gutt at the ende. kepe wele the blode. put the Laumprey on a ſpyt. rooſt hȳ ⁊ kepe wel the grece. grynde rayſons of corance. hȳ up ᶠ w̃ vyneg̃. wyne. and cruſt of brede. do þto powdo of gyng̃. of galyngale ᵍ. flo of canel. powdo of clow. and do þto raiſons of corance hoole. w þ blode ⁊ þ grece. ſeeþ it ⁊ ſalt it, boile it not to ſtondyng, take up the Laumprey do hȳ in a chargeo ʰ, ⁊ lay þ ſewe onoward, ⁊ ſue hȳ forth.

Laumprons in galyntyne.

Take Lamprons and ſcalde he. ſeeþ hem, meng powdo galyngale and ſome of the broth togyd ⁊ boile it ⁊ do þto powdo of gyng̃ ⁊ ſalt. take the Laumprons ⁊ boile he ⁊ lay he i dyſsh. ⁊ lay the ſewe above. ⁊ ſue fort.

Loſeyns ⁱ in Fyſsh Day.

Take Almand unblanched and waiſthe he clene, drawe he up with wat. ſeeþ þ mylke ⁊ alye it up w

---

ᶠ hȳ up. A word ſeems omitted; *drawe* or *lye*.
ᵍ of galyngale, i. e. powder. V. N° 101.
ʰ Chargeo'. charger or diſh. V. N° 127.
ⁱ Loſeyns. *Loſyns*, Contents.

loſeyns.

loſeyns. caſt þto ſafroñ. ſug̃. ⁊ ſalt ⁊ meſſe it forth with colyandre ĩ confyt rede, ⁊ ſũe it forth.

Sowp of galyntyne [k].

Take powdõ of galyngale with ſug̃ and ſalt and boile it yfere. take brede ytoſted. and lay the ſewe onoward. and ſũe it forth.

Sobre Sawſe.

Take Rayſoñs, grynde hem with cruſt of brede, and drawe it up with wyne. do þto goḍe powdõs and ſalt. and ſeeþ it. fry roch, looch, ſool, oþ ooþ gode Fyſsh, caſt þ ſewe above, ⁊ ſũe it forth.

Cold Brewet.

Take crome [l] of almañd. dry it in a cloth. and whan it is dryed do it in a veſſel, do þto ſalt, ſug̃, and white powdõ of gyng̃ and Juys of Fenel and wyne. and lat it wel ſtonde. lay full ⁊ meſſe ⁊ dreſſe it forth.

Peer [m] in confyt.

Take peer and pare hẽ clene. take gode rede wyne ⁊ mulberes [n] oþ ſañdꝛ and ſeeþ þ peer þin ⁊ whan þei

---

[k] Sowpes of Galyntyne. Contents has *in*, recte. *Sowpes* means Sops.   [l] crome. crumb, pulp.   [m] Peer. pears.
[n] mulberes. mulberries, for colouring.

buth

buth yſode, take hē up, make a ſyryp of wyne greke.
oþ vnage ° ẘ blaṅche powd͛ oþ white ſug̃ and powdõ
gyng̃ ₎ do the per̃ þin. ſeeþ it a lytel ₎ meſſe it
forth.

Egurdouce ᵖ of Fyſshe.   ^{xx.} VI. XIII.

Take Loch̃ oþ Tench̃ oþ Solys ſmyte hem on pecys.
fry hē in oyle. take half wyne half vyneg̃ and ſug̃ ₎
make a ſiryp. do þto oynoñs icorue ꝙ raiſoñs coraṅce.
and grete rayſoñs. do þto hole ſpices. gode powdõs
and ſalt. meſſe þ̇ fyſsh ₎ lay þ̇ ſewe aboue and ſũe
forth.

Colde Brewet.   ^{xx.} VI. XIIII.

Take Almañd and grynde hē. take the tweydel ͬ
of wyne oþ the þriddell of vyneg̃. drawe up the Almañd þẘ. take anys ſug̃ ₎ branch̃ of fenel grene a
fewe. ₎ drawe hē up togȳd ẘ þ mylke take poudõ
of canell. of gyng̃. cloŵ. ₎ maces hoole. take kydde
oþ chikeñs oþ fleſsh. ₎ choppe hem ſmall and ſeeþ
hem. take all þis fleſsh whan it is ſodeñ ₎ lay it ī a

° Vernage.   Vernaccia, a ſort of Italian white wine.   V. Gloſſ.
ᵖ Egurdouce.   Vide Gloſſ.
ꝙ icorue, icorven.   cut.   V. Gloſſ.
ͬ Tweydel.   Two parts.

clene

clene veſſel ꝺ boile þͧ ſewe ꝺ caſt þͧto ſalt. Ienne caſt
al þis in þͭ pot with fleſh. ꝺt.ͨ ˢ

Pevorat ᵗ for Veel and Venyſoñ.   xx. VI. XV.

Take Brede ꝺ fry it in grece. drawe it up with broth
and vyneg, take þͧto powdͧ of pep ꝺ ſalt and ſette it
on the fyre. boile it and meſſe it forth.

Sawſe ᵘ blañche for Capoñs yſode.   xx. VI. XVI.

Take Almandͧ blañched and grynd hem al to douſt.
temp it up with vions and powdͧ of gyngyñ and
meſſe it forth.

Sawſe Noyre for Capoñs yrofted.   xx VI. XVII.

Take the lyuͧ of Capons and rooſt it wel. take
anyſe and greynes de Parys ˣ. gyngͧ. canel. ꝺ a lytill
cruſt of brede and gͥnde it ſmale. and grynde it up
wͭ vions. and witþ grece of Capoñs. boyle it and ſue
it forth.

ˢ ꝺt. i. e. ſue forth.
ᵗ Pevorat. Peverade, from the pepper of which it is principally
compoſed.
ᵘ Sawſe. *Sawce*, Contents. As Nᵒ 137.
ˣ de Parys. Of Paradiſe. V. Pref.

Galyntyne.

Galyntyne ʸ.

xx.
VI. XVIII.

Take cruſt of Brede and grynde hem ſmale, do þto powdo of galyngale, of canel, of gyngyn and ſalt it, tempre it with vyneg and drawe it up þurgh a ſtrayno ⁊ meſſe it forth.

Gyngen ᶻ.

xx.
VI. XIX.

Take payndemayn and pare it clene and funde it in Vineg, grynde it and temp it wiþ Vyneg, and with powdo gyng and ſalt, drawe it thurgh a ſtyno. and ſue forth.

Verde ᵃ Sawſe.

xx.
VII.

Take pſel. mynt. garlek. a litul ſpell ᵇ and ſawge, a litul canel. gyng. pip. wyne. brede. vyneg ⁊ ſalt grynde it ſmal w ſafron ⁊ meſſe it forth.

Sawſe Noyre for Malard.

xx.
VII. I.

Take brede and blode iboiled. and grynde it and drawe it thurgh a cloth w Vyneg, do þto powdo of

---

ʸ Galyntyne. Galentyne, Contents.

ᶻ Gyngen. From the powder of Ginger therein uſed.

ᵃ Verde. It has the ſound of *Green-ſauce,* but as there is no Sorel in it, it is ſo named from the other herbs.

ᵇ a litul ſpell. Wild thyme.

I

gyng

gyng̃ ad of pep. ⁊ þͤ grece of the Maulard. ſalt it. boile it wel and sũe it forth.

Cawdel for Gees. xx. VII. II.

Take garlec and g̃nde it ſmale. Safron̄ and flo̾ þ̾- with ⁊ ſalt. and temp̱ it up with Cowe Mylke. and ſeeþ it wel and sũe it forth.

Chawdon̄ [c] for Swann̾ xx. VII. III.

Take þͤ lyu̾ and þͤ offall [d] of the Swann̾ ⁊ do it to ſeeþ ĩ gode broth. take it up. take out þͤ bonys. take ⁊ hewe the fleſsh ſmale. make a Lyo̾ of crust̾ of brede ⁊ of þͤ blode of þͤ Swan yſoden. ⁊ do þ̾to powdo̾ of clow̾ ⁊ of pip̱ ⁊ of wyne ⁊ ſalt, ⁊ ſeeþ it ⁊ caſt þͤ fleſsh þ̾to ihewed. and meſſe it forth wͭ þͤ Swan.

Sawſe Camelyne [e]. xx. VII. IIII.

Take Rayſon̄s of Corance. ⁊ kyrnels of notys. ⁊ crust̾ of brede ⁊ powdo̾ of gyng̃ clow̾ flo̾ of canel. bẏ it [f] wel togẏd and do it þ̾to. ſalt it, temp̱ it up with vyneg̃. and sũe it forth.

[c] Chawdōn. V. Gloſſ.
[d] offall. *Exta*, Gibles.
[e] Camelyne. Qu. if *Canelyne* from the *Fluor of Canel?*
[f] by. bray.

Lumbard

Lumbard Muſtard.   xx.
VII. v.

Take Muſtard ſeed and waiſhe it ⁊ drye it ĩ an
ovene, grynde it drye. ſarſe it thurgh a ſarſe. clarifie
hony w̃ wyne ⁊ vyneg̃ ⁊ ſtere it wel togedr̃ and make
it thikke ynowʒ. ⁊ whan p̃ wilt ſpende p̃of make it
thynne w̃ wyne.

Nota.   xx.
VII. VI.

Cranes ᵍ and Heroñs ſhul be armed ʰ with lard̃ of
Swyne. and eten with gyng̃.

Nota.   xx.
VII. VII.

Pokok and Ptruch ſhul be pboiled. lardid and
roſted. and eten with gyngeñ.

ᵍ Cranes. A diſh frequent formerly at great tables. Archæologia, II. p. 171. mentioned with Herons, as here, Mſ. Ed. 3.
where the ſame Recipe occurs. et 7. Lel. Coll. IV. p. 226. VI. p.
38. Rabelais, IV. c. 59. E. of Devon's Feaſt.

ʰ armed. Mſ. Ed. N° 3. has *enarmed*, as may be read there.
Enarmed, however, in Lel. Collect. IV. p. 225. means, decorated
with coate of arms. Sheldes of Brawn are there *in armor*, p. 226.
However, there is ſuch a word as *enorned*. Leland, p. 280. 285.
297. which approaches nearer.

        Fry

Fry blanched. XX. VII. VIII.

Take Almand blanched and grynde hē al to douſt, do þiſe ī a thynne foile. cloſe it þinne faſt. and fry it in Oile. clarifie hony w Wyne. & bake it þw.

Frytō of Paſternak of of Apples [i]. } XX. VII. IX.

Take ſkyrwaꝰ and paſtnak and apples, & pboile hē, make a batō of flō and ayreñ, caſt þto ale. ſafroñ & ſalt. wete hē ī þ batō and frye hē ī oile or ī grece. do þto Almañd Mylk. & ſue it forth.

Frytō of Mylke. XX. VII. X.

Take of crudd [k] and pſſe out þ wheyze [l]. do þto ſu whyte of ayreñ. fry hē. do þto. & lay on ſug and meſſe forth.

Frytō of Erbes. XX. VII. XI.

Take gode erbys. grynde hē and medle [m] hē w flō and wat & a lytel zeſt and ſalt, and frye hē ī oyle. and ete hē w clere hony.

---

[i] Frytour, &c. Contents has only, *Frytours of Paſternakes.* N. B. *Frytour* is *Fritter.*

[k] Cruddes. Curds, per metatheſin.

[l] wheyze. whey.   [m] medle. mix.

Raſyols.

Rasyols [n]. XX. VII. XII.

Take swyne lyuōs and seeþ hē wel. take brede & grate it. and take zolkes of ayreñ. & make hit sowple [o] and do þto a lytull of lard carnōn lyche a dee [p]. chese gtyd [q] &. whyte grece. powdō douce & of gyng & wynde it to ball [r] as grete as apples. take þ calle of þ swyne & cast eūe [s] by hȳ self þin. Make a Crust ī a trape [t]. and lay þ ball þin & bake it. and whan þey buth ynowȝ: put þin a layō of ayreñ w powdō fort and Safroñ. and sūe it forth.

Whyte Mylat [u]. XX. VII. XIII.

Take Ayreñ and wryng hē thurgh a cloth. take powdō fort, brede igrated, & safroñ, & cast þto a gode qntite of vyneg with a litull salt, medle all yfere. make a foile ī a trāp & bake it wel þinne. and sūe it forth.

[n] Rasyols. Rasiowls, Contents. Qu. the etymon.

[o] sowple. supple.

[p] carnōn lyche a dee. Cut like dice, diced. Fr. *De*; singular of *Dice*.

[q] gtyd. grated. *igrated*, N° 153.

[r] wynde it to balles, make it into Balls.

[s] eūe. each.

[t] trape. pan, or dish. French.

[u] Mylates. Contents, *Milates*; but 155 as here. Qu.

Cruſtard ⁹ ˣ of Fleſh.　XX. VII. XIIII⸴

Take peioñs ʸ　　　　and ſmaɪe brídd⁹
ſmyte hē ī gobett⁹　　wiþ ⁹viaws ᶻ do þto faf⸱
roñ, make a cruſt ī a trāp. and pynche it. ɛ cowche
þ fleſh þinne. ɛ caſt þinne Raiſoñs corance. powdo͐
douce and ſalt. breke ayreñ and wryɲg hem thurgh
a cloth ɛ ſwyng þ ſewe of þ　　　þw and helde
it ᵃ uppon the fleſh. coūe it ɛ bake it wel. and ſūe
it.forth.

Mylat ⁹ of Pork.　XX. VII. XV⸴

Hewe Pork al to pecys and medle it w̅ ͭ ayreñ ɛ
cheſe igted. do þto powdo͐ fort ſafroñ ɛ pyneꝛ ᵇ with
ſalt, make a cruſt ī, a trāp, bake it wel þinne, and ſūe
it forth⸱

Cruſtard ⁹ of Fyſhe.　XX. VII. XVI⸴

Take loch⁹, laumproñs, and Eelis. ſmyte hem on
pecys, and ſtewe hē wiþ Almañd Mylke and ⁹vions⸴
frye the loch ⁹ ī oile as tofore. and lay þ fiſh þinne⁹.

ˣ Cruſtards.　Pies.
ʸ peions.　pigeons.　V. ad Nᵒ 48⸱
ᶻ ⁹viaws.　Verjuice.
ᵃ helde it.　pour, caſt⸱
ᵇ pyneꝛ.　Vide Pref.

caſt þon powdo͛ fort powdo͛ douce. with rayſons corañce ⅋ prunes damyſyns. take galyntyn and þ ſewe
þinne, and ſwyng it togȳd and caſt ī the trape. ⅋
bake it and ſūe it forth.

Cru͛ſtard of Eerbis ᶜ on fyſsh Day. xx. vii. xvii.

Take gode Eerbys and grynde hē ſmale with walle-
not pyked clene. a grete portioñ. lye it up almoſt wiþ
as myche vions as waꝛ. ſeeþ it wel w powdo͛ and
Safroñ woute Salt. make a cruſt in a traꝓ and do þ
fyſsh þinne unſtewed wiþ a litel oile ⅋ gode Powdo͛.
whan it is half ybake do þ ſewe þto ⅋ bake it up.
If þ wilt make it clere of Fyſsh ſeeþ ayreñ harde. ⅋
take out þ zolk ⅋ gnde hē w gode powdo͛s. and alye
it up with gode ſtewes ᵈ and ſūe it forth.

Leſshes ᵉ fryed in lenton ᶠ. xx. vii. xviii.

Drawe a thick almañde Mylke wiþ waꝛ. take daꞇ
and pyke hē clene w apples and peer ⅋ mynce hē w
pnes damyſyns. take out þ ſtoñ out of þ pnes. ⅋
kerue the pnes a two. do þto Raiſoñs ſug. flo of canel. hoole macys and clow. gode powdo͛s ⅋ ſalt. colo͛

ᶜ Erbis. Rather *Erbis and Fiſch*.
ᵈ ſtewes. V. N° 170.
ᵉ Leſhes. V. Leche Lumbard in Gloſſ.
ᶠ lenton. Lentōn, Contents, i. e. Lent,

hem up w̆ fandr̃. meng þife with oile, make a coffyn
as þ dideſt bifor̃ ⁊ do þis Fars ᵍ þin. and bake it wel
and ſũe it forth.

Waſtels yfarced.

Take a Waſtel and hewe out þ crínnes. take ayren̄
⁊ ſhepis talow ⁊ þ crínn of þ ſame Waſtell powdõ
fort ⁊ ſalt w̆ Safron̄ and Raiſon̄s corañce. ⁊ medle alle
þiſe yfere ⁊ do it in þ Waſtel. cloſe it ⁊ bynde it faſt
togidre. and ſceþ it wel.

Sawge yfarced.

Take ſawge. gꞃynde it and temp it up with ayren̄.
a ſawcyſt ʰ ⁊ kerf hȳ to gobett and caſt it ĩ a poſſynet. and do ꝛwiþ grece ⁊ frye it. Whan it is fryed
ynowz caſt þto ſawge w̆ ayren make it not to harde.
caſt þto powdõ douce, meſſe it forth. If it be in
Ymber day: take ſauge butt ⁊ ayren̄. and lat it ſtonde
wel by þ ſauſe ⁱ, ⁊ ſũe it forth.

Sawgeat ᵏ.

Take Pork and ſeeþ it wel and gnde it ſmale and
medle it wiþ ayren ⁊ brede. ygrated. do þto powdõ

ᵍ Fars. Vide Gloſſ.   ʰ ſaweyſter. Qu.
ⁱ ſtonde wel by the ſauſe. Become thick with the ſawce.
ᵏ Sawgeat. So named from the Sage, or *Sawge*.

fort and fafroñ with pyñ ҩ falt. take ҩ clofe litull
Ball ī foiles ¹ of fawge. wete it with a batō of ayren
ҩ fry it. ҩ fūe it forth.

Cryfpes ᵐ.

Take flō of pandemayn and medle it with white
grece oủ the fyr in a chawfōⁿ and do the batō þto
queyntlich ° þurgħ þy fyngōs. or thurgh a fkymō.
and lat it a litul ᴾ quayle �q a litell fo þ þ be hool þinne.
And if þ wilt colō it wiþ alkenet yfoñdyt. take hē up
ҩ caft þinne fuǵ, and fūe hē forth.

Cryfpels.

Take and make a foile of gode Paft as thynne as
Pap. kerue it out ҩ fry it in oile. oþ, ī þ ʳ grece and

¹ foiles. leaves.

ᵐ Cryfpes. Mf. Ed. Nº 26. *Cryppys,* meaning *Crifps,* Chaucer
having *crips,* by tranfpofition, for *crifp.* In Kent *p* is commonly put
before the *f,* as *haps* is *hafp, waps* is *wafp.* V. Junius. V. *Happs,*
and *Haffe,* and *Wafp.*

ⁿ chawfō. chaffing difh.

° quentlich'. nicely.

ᴾ a litul. Dele.

q quayle. an cool?

ʳ þ grece. Dele *the.*

K   þ re-þ remnant [s], take hony clarified and flaunne [t] þw, alye hem up and sue hem forth.

Tartee. xx. VIII. IIII.

Take pork yfode. hewe it ⁊ bray it. do þto ayren. Raifons fug and powdo of gyng. powdo douce. and fmale bridd þamong ⁊ white grece. take prunes, faf-ron. ⁊ falt, and make a cruft i a trap ⁊ do þ Fars [u] þin. ⁊ bake it wel ⁊ sue it forth.

Tart in Ymbre [x] day. xx. VIII. V.

Take and pboile Oynons pffe out þ wat ⁊ hewe he fmale. take brede ⁊ bray it i a mort. and temp it up w Ayren. do þto butt. fafron and falt. ⁊ raifons corans. ⁊ a litel fug with powdo douce. and bake it i a trap. ⁊ sue it forth.

Tart de Bry [y]. xx. VIII. VI.

Take a Cruft ynche depe in a trap. take zolkes of Ayren rawe ⁊ chefe ruayn [z]. ⁊ medle it ⁊ þ zolkes to-

---

[s] þ remnant, i. e. as for the remnant.
[t] flaunne. French *flau*, cuftard.
[u] þ Fars, r. þ Fars.
[x] Ymbre. Ember.
[y] de Bry. Qu. *Brie*, the country.
[z] Chefe ruayn. Qu. of Roiſen. V. ad 49.

gyd.

gȳd. and do þto powdŏ gynḡ. ſuḡ. ſafroñ. and ſalt.
do it in a traꝑ, bake it and ſūe it forth.

Tart de brymlent ᵃ. XX.
VIII. VII.

Take Fyḡ ⁊ Rayſoñs. ⁊ waiſshe hē in Wyne. and
gnde hem ſmale w̃ apples ⁊ peŕ clene ypiked. take
hē up and caſt hē in a pot wiþ wyne and ſuḡ. take
ſalwar Salmōn ᵇ yſode. oꝑ codlyng, oꝑ haddok, ⁊
bray hē ſmal. ⁊ do þto white powdŏs ⁊ hool ſpices. ⁊
ſalt. and ſeeþ it. and whanne it is ſode ynowʒ. take
it up and do it in a veſſel and lat it kele. make a
Coffyn an ynche depe ⁊ do þ fars ꝑin. Plāñt it boueᶜ
w̃ prunes and damyſyns. take þ ſtoñ out, and wiþ
dates q̄rte redeᵈ and piked clene. and coūe the coffyn,
and bake it wel, and ſūe it forth.

Tartes of Fleſhᵉ. XX.
VIII. VIII.

Take Pork yſode and grynde it ſmale. tardeᶠ harde

ᵃ Brymlent. Perhaps Midlent or High Lent. *Bryme*, in Cotgrave, is the *midſt* of Winter. The fare is certainly lenten. A. S.
bꞃyme. Solennis, or beginning of Lent, from A. S. bꞃymm, ora,
margo. Yet, after all, it may be a miſtake for *Prymlent*.

ᵇ ſalwar Samōn. V. ad N° 98.

ᶜ plānt it above. Stick it *above*, or on the top.

ᵈ q̆rte red. quartered.

ᵉ Tartes of Fleſh. So we have *Tarte Poleyn*, Lel. Coll. IV.
p. 226. i. e. of Pullen, or Poultry.

ᶠ tarde, r. *take*. For ſee N° 169.

K 2   eyreñ

eyreñ ifode ⁊ ygrōnde and do ꝑto with Chefe ygronde.
take gode powdo and hool fpices, fug̃, fafroñ, and
falt ⁊ do ꝑto. make a coffyn as to feel fayde ᵍ ⁊ do þis
þinne, ⁊ plãnt it w̃ fmale bridd iftyned ⁊ cōnyng. ⁊
hewe hē to fmale gobett ⁊ bake it as tofore. ⁊ fūe it
forth.

Tartlet.   _{XX.}
VIII. IX.

Take Veel yfode and gnde it fmale. take harde
Eyreñ ifode and ygroñd ⁊ do ꝑto with prunes hoole ʰ.
dat. icorūe. pyñ and Raifoñs corañce. hool fpices ⁊
powdo. fug̃. falt, and make a litell coffyn and do þis
fars þinne. ⁊ bake it ⁊ fūe it forth.

Tart of Fyfshe.   _{XX.}
VIII. X.

Take Eelys and Samōn and fmyte hē on pecys. ⁊
ftewe it ⁱ ī almãnd mylke and vious. drawe up on
almãnd mylk wiþ þ ftewe. Pyke out the boñ clene of
þ fyfsh. and fave þ myddell pece hoole of þ Eelys ⁊
gnde þ ooþ fifsh fmale. and do ꝑto powdo, fug̃, ⁊ falt
and g̃ted brede. ⁊ fors þ Eelys þw þer as ᵏ þ bonys were
medle þ ooþ dele of the fars ⁊ þ mylk togiđ. and colo

ᵍ to feel fayde.   perhaps, *to hold the fame.*
ʰ hoole, whole.
ⁱ it.   rather *hem,* i. e. them.
ᵏ þeras.   where.   V. N° 177.

it

it ẘ ſañdr̊. make a cruſt in a trap as before. and bake
it þin and ſūe it forth.

Sambocade [1]. xx.
viii. xi.

Take and make a Cruſt ī a trap. ⁊ take a crudd
and wryng out þ̊ wheyze. and drawe hē þurgh a
ſtȳnŏ. and put ī þ ſtȳnŏ cruſt. do þto ſug̊ the þridde
part ⁊ ſomdel [m] whyte of Ayreñ. ⁊ ſhake þin blom
of elren [n]. ⁊ bake it up ẘ curoſe [o] ⁊ meſſe it forth.

Erbolat [p]. xx.
viii. xii.

Take pſel, mynt [q], ſauey, ⁊ ſauge, tanſey, vuayn,
clarry, rewe, ditayn, fenel, ſouthrenwode, hewe hē
⁊ gnde hē ſmale, medle hē up ẘ Ayreñ. do butt ī a
trap. ⁊ do þ fars þto. ⁊ bake it ⁊ meſſe it forth.

Nyſebek [r]. xx.
viii. xiii.

Take þe þridde part of ſowre Dokk and flŏ þto. ⁊
bete it toged tyl it be as towh as eny lyme. caſt þto

---

[1] Sambucade. As made of the *Sambucus*, or Elder.
[m] Somdel. Some.
[n] Blom of Elren. Elder flowers.
[o] curoſe.
[p] Erbolat, i. e. Herbolade, a confection of herbs.
[q] myntes, mint.
[r] Nyſebek. Qu.

ſalt.

falt. ⁊ do it ĩ a diſshe holke ˢ in þ̊ bothom, and let
it out wiþ þy fing̃ queynchche ᵗ ĩ a chowfer ᵘ wiþ
oile. ⁊ frye it wel. and whan it is ynowȝ : take it out
and caſt þ̊to ſug̃ ⁊c.

For to make Pom̃e Dorryle ˣ and oþ̊e þyng̃. ˣˣˑ
VIII.XIIII.

Take þ̊ lire of Pork rawe. and grynde it ſmale.
medle it up wiþ powdre fort, ſafroñ, and ſalt, and do
þ̊to Raiſoñs of Corañce, make ball þ̊of. and wete it
wele ĩ white of ayreñ. ⁊ do it to ſeeþ ĩ boillȳg waĩ.
take hem up and put hem on a ſpyt. roſt hẽ wel and
take þſel ygronde and wryng it up with ayren ⁊ a þty
of flõ. and lat erne ʸ abonte þ̊ ſpyt. And if þ̊ wilt, take
for þſel ſafroñ, and ſũe it forth.

ˢ holke. Qu. hollow.
ᵗ queynchche. an *queyntlich'*, as Nº 162.
ᵘ Chowfer. chaffing diſh, as Nº 162.
ˣ Pom̃e dorryle. Contents, *põ dorryes*, rectè, for MS. Ed. 42,
has *Pommedorry* ; and ſee Nº 177. So named from the *balls* and
the gilding. " Pommes dorées, golden apples." Cotgrave. *Põn-
dorroye.* MS. Ed. 58 ; but vide *Dorry* in Gloſſ.
ʸ erne. Qu.

Cotagres [z].

Take and make þ ſelf fars [a]. but do þto pyn and
ſug. take an hole rowſted cok, pulle hý [b] ᵹ hylde [c]
hym al togyd ſaue þ legg. take a pigg and hilde [d] hȳ
fro þ mydd doūward, fylle hī ful of þ fars ᵹ ſowe hȳ
faſt togid. do hȳ in a panne ᵹ ſeeþ hȳ wel and whan
þei bene iſode: do hē on a ſpyt ᵹ roſt it wele. colō
it w̱ zolkes of ayren and ſafroñ, lay þon foyles [e] of
gold and of ſilu. and ſūe hit forth.

Hert rowee [f].

Take þ mawe of þ grete Swyne. and fyſe oþ ſex
of pigg mawe. fyll hē full of þ ſelf fars. ᵹ ſowe hē
faſt, þboile hē. take hē up ᵹ make ſmale prews [g] of
gode paſt and frye hē. take þeſe þrews yfryed ᵹ ſeeþ [h]

---

[z] Cotagres.   This is a ſumptuous diſh.   Perhaps we ſhould read
Cokagres, from the *cock* and *grees*, or wild pig, therein uſed.   V.
vyne grace in Gloſſ.

[a] ſelf fars.   Same as preceding Recipe.

[b] pulle hȳ, i. e. in pieces.

[c] hylde.   caſt.

[d] hilde.   ſkin.

[e] foyles.   leaves; of Laurel or Bay, ſuppoſe; gilt and ſilvered
for ornament.

[f] Hert rowee.   Contents, *Hart rows*; perhaps from *heart*.

[g] prews.   Qu. V. in Gloſſ.

[h] ſeeþ.   There is a fault here, it means *ſtick*.

hē

hē þicke in þ̇ maw̆ on þ̇ fars made aft̃ⁱ an urchoñ
woute legg̊. put hem on a ſpyt ⁊ rooſt hē ⁊ coloˮ hèm
w̱ ſafroñ ⁊ meſſe hē forth.

Potews ᵏ.

Take Pottˮ of Erþ̇ lẏtell of half a quart and fẏll hem
full of fars of pōme dorryes ˡ. oþ̆ make with þyn
honde. oþ̆ ī a moolde pottˮ of þ̇ ſelf fars. put hem ī
wat̃ ⁊ ſeeþ hē up wel. and whan þey buth ynowȝ.
breke þ̇ pottˮ of erþ ⁊ do þ̇ fars on þ̇ ſpyt ⁊ roſt hē
wel. and whan þei buth yroſted. coloˮ hem as pōme
dorryes. make of litull prewes ᵐ gode paſt, frye hem
oþ̆ roſt hem wel ī grece. ⁊ make þ̆of Eerys ⁿ to pottˮ
⁊ coloˮ it. and make roſys ᵒ of gode paſt, ⁊ frye hē, ⁊
put þ̇ ſteles ᴾī þ̇ hole þ̆ᵠ þ̇ ſpyt was. ⁊ coloˮ it with
whyte. oþ̆ rede. ⁊ ſūe it forth.

ⁱ after, i. e. like.
ᵏ Potewṡ. probably from the *pots* employed.
ˡ pōme dorryes. Vide ad Nᵒ 174.
ᵐ prewes. V. ad 176.
ⁿ eerys. Ears *for* the pots. V. 185.
⁕ roſys. roſes.
ᴾ ſteles. ſtalks.
ᵠ þ̆. there, i. e. where. V. 170.

Sachus.

Sachus [r]. xx. VIII. XVIII.

Take fmale Sachellis of canuas and fille hem full of þ̊ fame fars [s] ⁊ feeþ hē. and whan þey buth ynowʒ take of the canvas. roft hem ⁊ colõ hem ⁊c.

Burfews [t]. xx. VIII. XIX.

Take Pork. feeþ it and grynde it fmale wiþ fodden ayren. do þ̊to gode powdõs and hole fpices and falt ẘ fuğ. make þ̊of fmale ball̊, and caft hē in a batõ [u] of ayren. ⁊ wete hē in flõ. and frye hē in grece as frytõs [x]. and fue hem forth.

Spynoch̊ [y] yfryed. xx. IX.

Take Spynoch̊. pboile hē ĩ feþyng wat̄. take hē up and pffe . . . out of þ̊ wat̄ [z] and hem [a] ĩ two. frye hē ĩ oile clene. ⁊ do þ̊to powdõ. ⁊ fue forth.

[r] Sachus. I fuppofe *facks*.

[s] fame fars. viz. as 174.

[t] Burfews. Different from *Burfen* in N° 11; therefore qu. etymon..

[u] Batõ. batter.

[x] frytõs. fritters.

[y] Spynoches. Spinage, which we ufe in the fingular.

[z] out of the water. dele *of*; or it may mean, *when out of the water*.

[a] hem r. *hewe*.

L   Benes

Benes yfryed.

Take benes and feeþ hē almoſt til þey berſten. take
and wryng out þ waſ clene. do þto Oynoñs yſode and
ymynced. and garlec þw. frye hem ī oile. oþ ī grece.
ҁ do þto powdo douce. ҁ sūe it forth.

Ryſshews [b] of Fruyt.

Take Fyg and raiſoñs. pyke hē and waiſshe hē in
Wyne. grynde hē wiþ apples and peerȝ ypared and
ypiked clene. do þto gode powdos. and hole ſpices.
make ball þof. fryē ī oile and sūe hē forth.

Daryols [c].

Take Creme of Cowe mylke. oþ of Almand. do þto
ayren w̄ ſug, ſafroñ, and ſalt. medle it yfere. do it ī a
coffyn. of 11. ynche depe. bake it wel and sūe it forth.

Flaumpeyns [d].

Take fat Pork yſode. pyke it clene. grynde it ſmale.
grynde Cheſe ҁ do þto. wiþ ſug and gode powdos.

---

b Ryſshews. *ruſhewſes*, Contents. Qu.

c Daryols. Qu.

d Flaumpeyns. *Flaumpens*, Contents. V. Nº 113.

make a coffyn of an ynche depe. and do þis fars þin.
make a thynne foile of gode paſt ꝭ kerue out poff
ſmale poynt ᵉ. frye hē in fars ᶠ. ꝭ bake it up ꝛꝇ.

Chewet ᵍ on Fleſshe Day.

Take þ lire of Pork and kerue it al to pecys. and
henn þwith and do it ī a panne and frye it ꝭ make a
Coffyn as to ʰ a pye ſmale ꝭ do þinne. ꝭ do þuppon
zolk of ayreñ. harde. powdo of gyng and ſalt, coue
it ꝭ fry it ī grece. oþ bake it wel and sūe it forth.

Chewet on Fyſsh Day.

Take Turbut. haddok. Codlyng. and hake. and
seeþ it. grynde it ſmale. and do þto Dat. ygronden.
rayſoñs pyñ. gode powdo and ſalt. make a Coffyn as
tofore ſaide. cloſe þis þin. and frye it ī oile. oþ ſtue
it in gyng. ſug. oþ ī wyne. oþ bake it. ꝭ sūe forth.

Haſtlet i of Fruyt.

Take Fyg iꝗrterid ᵏ. Rayſoñs hool dat and Almand

ᵉ Points, ſeems the ſame as *Prews*, N° 176.

ᶠ in fars, f. *in the fars*; and yet the Fars is diſpoſed of before;
ergo quære.

ᵍ Chewets. V. 186.　　　ʰ as to, as for. V. N° 177.

ⁱ Haſtletes. *Haſteletes*, Contents.

ᵏ iꝗrterid. iquartered.

　　　　　　hoole.

hoole. and ryne[1] hē on a ſpyt and rooſt hē. and endore[m] hem as pōme dorryes ⁊ ſūe hē forth.

xx.
ix. vii.

Comadore[n].

Take Fyg and Raiſoñs. pyke hem and waiſshe hē
clene. ſkalde hē ī wyne. grynde hē right ſmale. caſt
ſug ī þ ſelf wyne. and ſoñde it togȳd. drawe it up
thurgh a ſtynō. ⁊ alye up þ fruyt þw. take gode
peerys and Appl. pare hem and take þ beſt, grynde
hem ſmale and caſt þto. ſet a pot on þ fuyr[o] wiþ
oyle and caſt alle þiſe þyng þinne. and ſtere it warliche,
and kepe it wel fro brēnyng. and whan it is fyned
caſt þto powdōs of gyng of canel. of galyngale. hool
clow flō of canel. ⁊ macys hoole. caſt þto pyn a litel
fryed ī oile ⁊ ſalt, and whan it is ynowȝ fyned. take
it up and do it ī a veſſel ⁊ lat it kele. and whan it is
colde. kerue out w a knyf ſmale pecys of þ gretneſſe
⁊ of þ length of a litel fyng. ⁊ cloſe it faſt ī gode
paſt. ⁊ frye hē ī oile. ⁊ ſūe forth.

---

[1] ryne. run.
[m] endore. endorſe, MS. Ed. 42. II. 6. v. ad 147.
[n] Comadore. Qu.
[o] Fuyr. fire.

Chaſtle

Chaftlet[p].   xx,
                                            IX. IX.

Take and make a foyle of gode paſt with a roller
of a foot brode. ⁊ lyng[q] by cūpas. make iiii Coffyns
of þ ſelf paſt uppon þ roller þ gretneſſe of þ ſmale of
þyn Arme. of vi ynche depneſſe. make þ gretuſt[r] ī
þ myddell. faſten þ foile ī þ mouth upwarde. ⁊ faſten
þee[s] oþe foure ī euy ſyde. kerue out keyntlich kyrnels[t] above ī þ mane of bataiwyng[u] and drye hē harde
ī an Ovene. oþ ī þ Sūne. In þ myddel Coffyn do a
fars of Pork w̄ gode Pork ⁊ ayrēn rawe wiþ ſalt. ⁊
coloͬ it wiþ ſafron and do in anoþ Creme of Almand.
and helde[x] it in anoþ[y] creme of Cowe mylke w̄ ayrēn.
coloͬ it w̄ ſandͬ.   anoþ man. Fars of Fyg. of ray-
ſōns. of Apples. of Peer. ⁊ holde it in brōn[z]. anoþ

---

[p] Chaftelets. Little caſtles, as is evident from the kernelling and
the battlements mentioned. *Caftles of jelly templewife made.* Lel.
Coll. IV. p. 227.

[q] lyng. longer.

[r] gretūſt. greateſt.

[s] þee, i. e. thou.

[t] kyrnels. Battlements. **V. Gloſſ.** Keyntlich, quaintly, curiouſly. **V. Gloſſ.**

[u] bataiwyng. embatteling.

[x] helde. put, caſt.

[y] another. As the middle one and only two more are provided
for, the two remaining were to be filled, I preſume, in the ſame
manner alternately.

[z] holde it brōn. make it brown.

                                            manē.

manē. do fars as to frytos blanched. and colo̅ it with grẹne. put þis to þ ovene ȼ bake it wel. ȼ sūe it forth w ẹw ardant [a].

For to make 11. [b] pecys of Flefsh }
to faften togȳd. } xx. IX. X.

Take a pece of frefsh Flẹfh and do it ī a pot for to feeþ. oꝛ take a pece of frefsh Flefsh and kerue it al to gobet. do it ī a pot to feeþ. ȼ take þ wofe [c] of comfery ȼ put it ī þ pot to þ flefsh ȼ it fhal faftē ano̅, ȼ fo sūe it forth.

Pur fait Ypocras [d]. xx. IX. XI.

Treys Unces de caneꝉ. ȼ iij unces de gyngen. fpykenard de Spayn le pays dun dener [e]. garyngale [f]. clowes, gylofre. pocur long [g], noiez mugadez [h]. ma-

[a] ew ardānt. hot water. *Eau*, water; anciently written *eue.*

[b] 11. *Twey*, Contents.

[c] wofe. Roots of comfrey arẹ of a very glutinous nature. Qùincy, Difpenf. p. 100. *Wofe* is A. S. pæꝛ, *bumour*, juice. See Junius, v. *Wos*, and Mr. Strype's Life of Stow, p. VIII.

[d] Pur fait Ypocras. Id eft, *Pour faire Ypocras*; a whole pipe of which was provided for archbifhop Nevill's feaft about A. D. 1466. So that it was in vaft requeft formerly.

[e] le pays d'un dener, i. e. *le poys d'un Denier.*

[f] garyngale, i. e. *galyngale.*

[g] pocur long, r. poiur long, i. e. *poivre long.*

[h] mugadez, r. mufcadez; but q. as the French is *muguette.* Nutmegs.

ziozame

ziozame ⁱ cardemonij ^k de chefcuñ i. q̃rt' douce ^l grayne
ꝗ ^m de paradys flo̅ de queynel ⁿ de chefcuñ di̅ ^o unce de
tout. foit fait powdo̅ ꝗc.

For to make blank mañg ^p.   xx.
IX. XII.

Put Rys i̅ wat̅ al a nyȝt and at morowe waifshe he̅
clene. aft̅ward put he̅ to þ fyr̅ fort ^q þ̇ þey berft ꝗ not
to myche. ffithen ^r take brawn of Capoñs, or of henn̅.
foden ꝗ drawe ^s it fmale. aft̅ take mylke of Almand̅.
and put i̅ to þ̇ Ryys ꝗ boile it. and whan it is yboiled
put i̅ þ̇ brawn ꝗ alye it þwith. þ̇ it be wel chargeañt ^t
and mung it fynelich ^u wel þ̇ it fit not ^x to þ̇ pot. and
whan it is ynowȝ ꝗ chargeañt. do þto fug̅ gode part,
put þin almand̅. fryed i̅ white grece. ꝗ dreffe it forth.

ⁱ maziozame, r. *marjorame.*
^k Cardemonij, r. *Cardamones.*
^l 1 q̃rtdouce, r. *d'once.* Five penny weights.
^m ꝗ. dele.
ⁿ queynel. Perhaps *Capell;* but qu. as that is named before.
^o dj̅. dimid.
^p blank mañg. Very different from that we make now. V. 36.
^q fyr̅ fort. ftrong fire.
^r ffithen. then.
^s drawe. make.
^t chargeant. ftiff. So below, *ynowhz & chargeañt.* V. 193,
194. V. Gloff.
^u mung it fynelich' wel. ftir it very well.
^x fit not. adheres not, and thereby burns not. Ufed now in the
North.

For

For to make blank Defne [y].   XX.
IX. XIII.

Take Brawn of Henñ or of Capoñs yſodẽ withoute þ ſkyn. ⁊ hewe hẽ as ſmale as þ may. ⁊ gnde
hem ĩ a mort. afṫ take gode mylke of Almand ⁊ put
þ brawn þin. ⁊ ſtere it wel togyd ⁊ do hem to ſeeþ.
⁊ take flo of Rys ⁊ amydoñ ⁊ alay it. ſo þat it be
chargeant. ⁊ do þto ſug a gode pty. ⁊ a pty of white
grece. and when it is put ĩ diſsh ſtrewe uppon it
blanche powdo. and þenne put in blank deſire and
mawmenye ĩ diſshes togider. and ſue forth.

For to make Mawmenny [a].   XX.
IX. XIIII.

Take þ cheſe and of Fleſsh of Capoñs or of Henñ.
⁊ hakke ſmale iñ a mort. take mylke of Almand w þ
broth of freiſsh Beef, oþ freiſsh fleſsh. ⁊ put the fleſsh
ĩ þ mylke oþ in the broth and ſet hẽ to þ frye [b]. ⁊
alye hẽ up w floo of Ryſe. or gaſtbon [c]. or amydoñ.
as chargeant as þ blanke deſire. ⁊ w zolk of ayren and

---

[y] blank *Defne*. *Defire*, Contents; recte. V. Gloſſ. The Recipe
in MS. Ed. 29 is much the ſame with this.

[z] Mawmenye. See N[d] 194.

[a] Mawmenny. *Mawmoune*, Contents. *Maumene*, MS. Ed. 29.
30. vide N° 193. See Preface for a *fac-ſimile* of this Recipe.

[b] þ frye. an fyre?

[c] gaſtbon. Qu.

I   ſafroñ

ſafroñ for to make it zelow. and when it is dreſſit in diſsh ẘ blank deſir̊ ſtyk above cloẘ de gilofre. ẻ ſtrewe Powdo̊ of galyngale above. and ſue it forth.

The Pety Puãnt ^d.

xx.
IX. XV.

Take malė Marow ^e. hole parade ^f and kerue it rawe. powdo̊ of Gyng̊. zolk̊ of Ayreñ, dat mynced. raiſoñs of corañce. ſalt a lytel. ẻ loke þ̓ þ̈ make þy paſt with zolkes of Ayren. ẻ þat no waᵗ come þto. and fome þy coffyn. and make up þy paſt.

Payn puff ^g.

xx.
IX. XVI.

Eodem m̊ fait payn puff. but make it more tendre þ̈ paſt. and loke þ̊ paſt be roñde of þ̊ payn puf as a coffyn ẻ a pye.

^h 𝔵𝔭𝔩𝔦𝔠𝔦𝔱.

^d pety puãnt. a paſte; therefore, perhaps, *paty*; but qu. the latter word.

^e male Marow. Qu.

^f parade. Qu.

^g Payn puff. Contents has, *And the pete puant.*

^h A blank was left in the original for a large *F.*

M

The

The following Memorandum at the End of the Roll.

" Antiquum huc monumentum oblatum et miſſum eſt majeſtati veſtræ vicefimo feptimo die menfis Julij, anno regno veſtri fæliciſſimi vicefimo viij ab humilimo veſtro ſubdito, veſtræq̃ majeſtati fideliſſimo

E^D STAFFORD,
Hæres domus fubverſæ Buckinghamienſ."

N.B. He was Lord Stafford and called Edward.

Edw. D. of Bucks beheaded 1521.   13 H. VIII.
|
Henry, reſtored in blood by H. VIII.; and again
| [1 Ed. VI.
Edw. aged 21, 1592; born 1592. 21. ob. 1525.
| 21   [f. 1625.
Edw. b. 1600.   ———
             1571 born.

ANCIENT COOKERY.

A. D. 1381.

*Hic incipiunt univerſa ſervicia tam de
carnibus quam de piſſibus*[a]*:*

I. For to make Furmenty [a].

NYM clene Wete and bray it in a morter wel
that the holys [b] gon al of and ſeyt [c] yt til it
breſte and nym yt up. and lat it kele [d] and nym fayre
freſch broth and ſwete mylk of Almandys or ſwete
mylk of kyne and temper yt al. and nym the yolkys
of eyryn [e]. boyle it a lityl and ſet yt adõn and meſſe
yt forthe wyth fat venyſon and freſh moton.

---

[a] See again, Nº I. of the ſecond part of this treatiſe.
[b] Hulls.
[c] Miſwritten for *ſcyth* or *ſethe*, i. e. ſeeth.
[d] cool.
[e] eggs.

M 2   II.

II. For to make Pife of Almayne.

Nym wyte Pifyn and wafch hem and feth hem a good wyle fithfyn wafch hem in golde [f] watyr unto the holys gon of alle in a pot and kever it wel that no breth paffe owt and boyle hem ryzt wel and do therto god mylk of Almandys and a party of flowr of ris and falt and fafron and meffe yt forthe.

III.

Cranys and Herons fchulle be euarud [g] wyth Lardons of fwyne and roftyd and etyn wyth gyngynyr.

IV.

Pecokys and Partrigchis fchul ben yparboyld and lardyd and etyn wyth gyngenyr.

V. Morterelys [h].

Nym hennyn and porke and feth hem togedere nym the lyre [i] of the hennyn and the porke and hakkyth fmale and grynd hit al to duft and wyte bred therwyth and temper it wyth the felve broth and wyth heyryn and colure it with fafron and boyle it and difch it and caft theron powder of peper and of gyngynyr and ferve it forthe.

---

[f] cold.

[g] Perhaps *enarmed*, or *enorned*. See Mr. Brander's Roll, N° 146.

[h] V. Mortrews in Gloff.   [i] Flefh.

VI.

VI. Caponys in concys.

Schal be ſodyn. Nym the lyre and brek it ſmal in a morter and peper and wyte bred therwyth and temper it wyth ale and ley it wyth the capoñ Nym hard ſodyn eyryn and hewe the wyte ſmal and kaſte thereto and nym the zolkys al hole and do hem in a dyſch and boyle the capoñ and colowre it wyth ſafroñ and ſalt it and meſſe it forthe.

VII. Hennys [k] in bruet.

Schullyn be ſcaldyd and ſodyn wyth porke and grynd pepyr and comyn bred and ale and temper it wyth the ſelve broth and boyle and colowre it wyth ſafroñ and ſalt it and meſſe it forthe.

VIII. Harys [l] in cmee [m].

Schul be parboylyd and lardyd and roſtid and nym onyons and myce hem rizt ſmal and fry hem in wyte gres and grynd peper bred and ale and the onions therto and coloure it wyth ſafroñ and ſalt it and ſerve it forth.

IX. Haris in Talbotays.

Schul be hewe in gobbettys and ſodvn with al the blod Nym bred piper and ale and grynd togedere

[k] Hens. [l] Hares.

[m] Perhaps *Cinee*; for ſee Nᵒ 51.

and

and temper it with the felve broth and boyle it and falt it and ferve it forthe.

X. Conynggys,[n] in Gravey.

Schul be fodyn and hakkyd in gobbettys and grynd gyngynyr galyngale and canel. and temper it up with god almand mylk and boyle it and nym macys and clowys and keft [o] therin and the conynggis alfo and falt hym [p] and ferve it forthe.

XI. For to make a Colys [q].

Nym hennys and fchald hem wel. and feth hem after and nym the lyre and hak yt fmal and bray it with otyn grotys in a morter and with wyte bred and temper it up wyth the broth Nym the grete bonys and grynd hem al to duft and keft hem al in the broth and mak it thorw a clothe and boyle it and ferve it forthe.

XII. For to make Nombles [r].

Nym the nomblys of the venyfon and wafch hem clene in water and falt hem and feth hem in tweye waterys grynd pepyr bred and ale and temper it wyth the fecunde brothe and boyle it and hak the nomblys and do theryn and ferve it forthe.

---

[a] Rabbits.
[p] *it*, or perhaps *hem*.
[r] Umbles.

[o] Caft.
[q] Cullis. V. Preface.

XIII.

XIII. For to make blanché Brewet de Alyngyn.

Nym kedys ⁵ and chekenys and hew hem in mor-
fellys and feth hem in almand mylk or in kyne mylke
grynd gyngyncr galingale and caft therto and boyle
it and ferve it forthe.

XIV. For to make Blomanger ᵗ.

Nym rys and lefe hem and wafch hem clene and do
thereto god almande mylk and feth hem tyl they al to
breft and than lat hem kele and nym the lyre of the
hennyn or of capoñs and grynd hem fmal keft therto
wite grefe and boyle it Nym blanchyd almandys and
fafroñ and fet hem above in the dyfche and ferve yt
forthé.

XV. For to make Afronchemoyle ᵘ.

Nym eyren wyth al the wyte and myfe bred and
fchepys ʷ talwe as grét as dyfes ˣ grynd peper and
fafroñ and caft therto and do hit in the fchepis wombe
feth it wel and dreffe it forthé of brode leches thynne.

---

⁵ Kids.

ᵗ Blanc-manger. See again, N° 33, 34. II. N° 7. Chauc
writes it *Blankmanger.*

ᵘ Frenchemulle d'un mouton. A fheeps call, or kell. Cotgra\
Junius, v. *Moil,* fays, " a French moile Chaucero eft cibus deli.
" tior, a difh made of marrow and grated bread."

ʷ Sheep's fat.

ˣ dice; fquare bits, or bits as big as dice.

XVI.

XVI. For to make Brymeus.

Nym the tharmys [y] of a pygge and wafch hem clene in water and falt and feth hem wel and than hak hem fmale and grynd pepyr and fafroñ bred and ale and boyle togedere Nym wytys of eyryñ and knede it wyth flour and mak fmal pelotys [z] and fry hem with wyte grees and do hem in difches above that othere mete and ferve it forthe.

XVII. For to make Appulmos [a].

Nym appelyn and feth hem and lat hem kele and make hem thorw a clothe and on flefch dayes kaft therto god fat breyt [b] of Bef and god wyte grees and fugar and fafroñ and almande mylk on fyfch dayes oyle de olyve and gode powdres [c] and ferve it forthe.

XVIII. For to make a Froys [d].

Nym Veel and feth it wel and hak it fmal and grynd bred peper and fafroñ and do thereto and frye yt and preffe it wel upon a bord and dreffe yt forthe.

---

[y] Rops, guts, puddings.
[z] Balls, pellets, from the French *pelote*.
[a] See N° 35.
[b] Breth, i. e. broth. See N° 58.
[c] Spices ground fmall. See N° 27, 28. 35. 58. II. N° 4. 17. or perhaps of Galingale. II. 20. 24.
[d] a Fraife.

XIX.

XIX. For to make Fruturs [e].

Nym flowre and eyryn and grynd peper and fafroñ and mak therto a batour and par aplyn and kyt hem to brode penys [f] and keſt hem theryn and fry hem in the batour wyth freſch grees and ſerve it forthe.

XX. For to make chanke [g].

Nym Porke and ſeth it wel and hak yt ſmal nym eyryn wyth al the wytys, and ſwyng hem wel al togedere and kaſt god ſwete mylke thereto and boyle yt and meſſe it forthe.

XXI. For to make Juffel.

Nym eyryn wyth al the wytys and mice bred grynd pepyr and fafroñ and do therto and temper yt wyth god freſch broth of porke and boyle it wel and meſſe yt forthe.

XXII. For to make Gees [h] in ochepot [i].

Nym and ſchald hem wel and hew hem wel in gobettys al rawe and ſeth hem in her owyn grees and caſt therto wyn or ale a cuppe ful and myce onyons ſmal and do tnerto and boyle yt and falt yt and meſſe yt forthe.

---

[e] Fritters. [f] Pieces as broad as pennies, or perhaps pecys.
[g] Quære. [h] Geele.
[i] Hochepot. Vide Gloſſ.

XXIII.

XXIII. For to make eyryn in bruet.

Nym water and welle ^k yt and brek eyryn and kaſt
theryn and grynd peper and ſafroñ and temper up
wyth ſwete mylk and boyle it and hakke cheſe ſmal
and caſt theryn and meſſe yt forthe.

XXIV. For to make craytoñ ^l.

Tak checonys and ſchald hem and ſeth hem and
grynd gyngen' other pepyr and comyn and temper it
up wyth god mylk and do the checonys theryn and
boyle hem and ſerve yt forthe.

XXV. For to make mylk roſt.

Nym ſwete mylk and do yt in a panne nyn ^m eyryn
wyth al the wyte and ſwyng hem wel and caſt therto
and colowre yt wyth ſafroñ and boyl it tyl yt wexe
thykke and thanne ſeth ⁿ yt thorw a culdore ^o and nym
that levyth ^p and preſſe yt up on a bord and wan yt
ys cold larde it and ſcher yt on ſchyverys and roſte
yt on a grydern and ſerve yt forthe.

---

^k Quære the meaning.
^l Vide ad N° 60 of the Roll.
^m Read *nym*.
ⁿ ſtrain. See N° 27.
^o Cullinder.
^p That which is left in the cullinder.

3

XXVI.

XXVI. For to make cryppys q.

Nym flour and wytvs of eyryn fugur other hony and fweyng togedere and mak a batour nym wyfe grees and do yt in a pofnet and caft the batur there-yn and ftury to thou have many r and tak hem up and meffe hem wyth the frutours and ferve forthe.

XXVII. For to make Berandyles s.

Nym Hennys and feth hem wyth god Buf and wan hi ben fodyn nym the Hennyn and do awey the bonys and bray final yn a mortar and temper yt wyth the broth and feth yt thorw a culdore and caft therto powder of gyngenyr and fugur and graynys of pow-mis gernatys t and boyle yt and dreffe yt in dyfches and caft above clowys gylofres u and maces and god powder x ferve yt forthe.

XXVIII. For to make capons in caffelys.

Nym caponys and fchald hem nym a penne and opyn the fkyn at the hevyd y and blowe hem tyl the fkyn ryfe from the flefshe and do of the fkyn al hole

q Meaning, *crips*. V. Gloff.

r It will run into lumps, I fuppofe.

s Quære the meaning.

t Pomegranates. V. N° 39.

u Not clove-gilliflowers, but *cloves*. See N° 30, 31, 40.

x See N° 17, note c.

y Head. Sax. heoꝛoꝺ and hevoꝺ, hence our *Head*.

and

and feth the lyre of Hennyn and zolkys of heyryn
and god powder and make a Farfure [z] and fil ful the
fkyn and parboyle yt and do yt on a fpete and roft
yt and droppe [a] yt wyth zolkys of eyryn and god
powder roftyng and nym the caponys body and larde
yt and rofte it and nym almaunde mylk and amydon [b]
and mak a batur and droppe the body roftyng and
ferve yt forthe.

XXIX. For to make the blank furry [c].

Tak brann [d] of caponys other of hennys and the
thyes [e] wythowte the fkyn and kerf hem fmal als
thou mayft and grynd hem fmal in a morter and tak
mylk of Almaundys and do yn the branne and grynd
hem thanne togedere and and feth hem togeder' and
tak flour of rys other amydon and lye it that yt be
charchant and do therto fugur a god parti and a
party of wyt grees and boyle yt and wan yt ys don
in dyfchis ftraw upon blank poudere and do togedere
blank de fury and manmene [f] in a dyfch and ferve it
forthe.

---

[z] ftuffing.
[a] bafte.
[b] Vide Gloff.
[c] Vide *Blank Defire* in Gloff.
[d] Perhaps *brawn*, the brawny part.   See N° 33. and the Gloff.
[e] Thighs.
[f] See the next number.   Quære *Mawmeny*.

XXX.

XXX. For to make manmene [g].

Tak the thyys [h] other the flefch of the caponys
fede [i] hem and kerf hem fmal into a morter and tak
mylk of Almandys wyth broth of frefch Buf and do
the flefch in the mylk or in the broth and do yt to
the fyre and myng yt togedere wyth flour of Rys
othere of waftelys als charchaut als the blank de fure
and wyth the zolkys of eyryn for to make it zelow
and fafroñ and wan yt ys dreffyd in dyfches wyth
blank de fure ftraw upon clowys of gelofre [k] and ftraw
upon powdre of galentyn and ferve yt forthe.

XXXI. For to make Bruet of Almayne.

Tak Partrichys roftyd and checonys and qualys
roftyd and larkys ywol and demembre the other and
mak a god cawdel and dreffe the flefch in a dyfch
and ftrawe powder of galentyn therupon. ftyk upon
clowys of gelofre and ferve yt forthe.

XXXII. For ro make Bruet of Lombardye.

Tak chekenys or hennys or othere flefch and mak
the colowre als red as any blod and tak peper and
kanel and gyngyner bred [l] and grynd hem in a morter

[g] Vide Number 29, and the Gloff.
[h] Thighs.
[i] Quære.
[k] See N° 27, note [u].
[l] This is ftill in ufe, and, it feems, is an old compound.

and

and a porçon of bred and mak that bruer thenne and do that flefch in that broth and mak hem boyle to-gedere and ftury it wel and tak eggys and temper hem wyth Jus of Parcyle and wryng hem thorwe a cloth and wan that bruet is boylyd do that therto and meng tham togedere wyth fàyr greês fo that ÿt be fat ynòw and fervé yt forthe.

XXXIII. For to make Blomanger [m].

Do Ris in water al nyzt and upon the morwe wafch hem wel and do hem upon the fyre for to [n] they breke and nozt for to muche and tak Brann [o] of Caponıs foôyn and wel ydraw [p] and fmal and tak almaund mylk and boyle it wel wyth ris and wan it is yboylyd do the flefch therin fo that it be charghaunt and do therto a god party of fugure and wan it ys dreffyd forth in difchis ftraw theron blaunche Poudèr and ftrik [q] theron Almaundys fryed wyt wyte grece [r] and ferve yt forthe.

XXXIV. For to make Sandale that party to Blomanger.

Tak Flefch of Caponys and of Pork foôyn kerf yt fmal into a morter togedere and bray that wel. and

[m] See N° 14.

[n] till. *for*, however, abounds.

[o] See N° 29. note [d].

[p] Perhaps, *ftrained*. See N° 49; and Part II. N° 33.

[q] Perhaps, *ftik*, i. e. ftick; but fee 34.

[r] Grefe. Fat, or lard.

temper

temper it up wyth broth of Caponys and of Pork
that yt be wel charchaunt alſo the crem of Almaundys
and grynd egg⁹ and ſafron or ſandres togedere that it
be coloured and ſtraw upon Powder of Galentyn
and ſtrik thereon clowys and maces and ſerve it
forthe.

XXXV. For to make Apulmos ˢ.

Tak Applys and ſeth hem and let hem kele and
after mak hem thorwe a cloth and do hem in a pot and
kaſt to that mylk of Almaundys wyth god broth of
Buf in Fleſch dayes do bred ymyed ᵗ therto. And
the fiſch dayes do therto oyle of olyve and do therto
ſugur and colour it wyth ſafron and ſtrew theron
Powder and ſerve it forthe.

XXXVI. For to make mete Gelee ᵘ that it be wel chariaunt.

Tak wyte wyn and a party of water and ſafron
and gode ſpicis and fleſch of Piggys or of Hennys or
freſch Fiſch and boyle them togedere and after wan
yt ys boylyd and cold dres yt in diſchis and ſerve yt
forthe.

ˢ See Nº 17.
ᵗ f. ymyced, i, e. *minced.*
ᵘ meat jelly.

XXXVII. For to make Murrey [x].

Tak mulbery [y] and bray hem in a morter and wŋyng [z] hem thorth a cloth and do hem in a pot over the fyre and do ther'to fat bred and wyte greſſe and let it nazt boyle no ofter than onys and do ther'to a god party of ſugur and zif yt be nozt ynowe colowrd brey mulburus and ferve yt forthe.

XXXVIII. For to make a penche of Egges.

Tak water and do it in a panne to the fyre and lat yt fethe and after tak eggs and brek hem and caſt hem in the water and after tak a chefe and kerf yt on fowr partins and caſt in the water and wanne the chefe and the eggys ben wel fodyn tak hem owt of the water and wafch hem in clene water and tak waſtel breed and temper yt wyth mylk of a kow. and after do yt over the fyre and after forfy yt wyth gyngener and wyth comyn and colowr yt wyth faf-ron and lye yt wyth eggys and oyle the fewe wyth Boter and kep wel the chefe owt and dreſſe the fewe and dymo [a] eggys ther'on al ful and kerf thy chefe in lytyl fchyms and do hem in the fewe wyth eggys and ferve yt forthe.

---

[x] Morrey. Part II. N° 26.

[y] This is to be underſtood pluraly, *quaſi* mulberries.

[z] Read *wryng*. For fee part II. N° 17. 28. Chaucer, v. *wronge* and *ywrong*.

[a] Perhaps, *do mo*, i. e. put more.

XXXIX. For to make Comyn.

Tak god Almaunde mylk and lat yt boyle and do ther'in amydon wyth flowr of Rys and colowr yt wyth fafron and after dreffe yt wyth graynis of Poungarnetts ^b other wyth reyfens zyf thow haft non other and tak fugur and do theryn and ferve it forthe.

XIV. For to make Fruturs ^c.

Tak crommys ^d of wyte bred and the flowris of the fwete Appyltre and zolkys of Eggys and bray hem togedere in a morter and temper yt up wyth wyte wyn and mak yt to fethe and wan yt is thykke do thereto god fpicis of gyngener galyngale canel and clowys gelofre and ferve yt forth.

XLI. For to make Rofee .

Tak the flowris of Rofys and wafch hem wel ih water and after bray hem wel in a morter and than tak Almondys and temper hem and feth hem and after tak flefch of capons or of hennys and hac yt fmale and than bray hem wel in a morter and than do yt in the Rofe ^f fo that the flefch acorde wyth the mylk and fo that the mete be charchaunt and after do yt to the fyre to boyle and do thereto fugur and fafron

---

^b Vide N° 27   ^c Fritters.
^d Crumbs.   ^e Vide N° 47.
^f i. e. Rofee.

O   that

that yt be wel ycolowrd and rofy of levys and of the forfeyde flowrys and ferve yt forth.

XLII. For to make Pommedorry [g].

Tak Buff and hewe yt fmal al raw and caft yt in a morter and grynd yt nozt to fmal tak fafroñ and grynd ther'wyth wan yt ys grounde tak the wyte of the eyryn zyf yt be nozt ftyf. Caft into the Buf pouder of Pepyr olde refyns and of coronfe fet over a panne wyth fayr water and mak pelotys of the Buf and wan the water and the pelots ys wel yboylyd and [h] fet yt adon and kele yt and put yt on a broche and roft yt and endorre yt wyth zolkys of eyryn and ferve yt forthe.

XLIII. For to make Longe de Buf [i].

Nym the tonge of the rether [k] and fchalde and fchawe [l] yt wel and rizt clene and feth yt and fethe nym a broche [m] and larde yt wyth lardons and wyth clowys and gelofr' and do it roftyng and drop yt wel yt roftyd [n] wyth zolkys of eyrin and dreffe it forthe.

---

[g] Vide N° 58.

[h] dele *and*.

[i] Neat's Tongue. *Make* fignifies *to drefs*, as II. 12.

[k] The ox or cow. Lye in Jun. Etymolog. v. *Rother*.

[l] Shave, fcrape.

[m] A larding-pin.

[n] Pehaps, *wyle it roftyth*.

XLIV.

XLIV. For to make Rew de Rumſy.

Nym ſwynys fet and eyr[o] and make hem clene and ſeth hem alf wyth wyn and half wyth water caſt mycyd onyons ther'to and god ſpicis and wan they be yſodyn nym and roſty hem iñ a gryder' wan it is yroſtyd keſt thereto of the ſelve broth hy lyed wyth amydoñ and anyeyd onyons[p] and ſerve yt forth.

XLV. For to make Bukkenade[q].

Nym god freſch fleſch wat maner ſo yt be and hew yt in ſmale morſelys and ſeth yt wyth gode freſch buf and caſt ther'to gode mynced onyons and gode ſpiceryе and alyth[r] wyth eyryn and boyle and dreſſe yt forth.

XLVI. For to make ſpine[s].

Nym the flowrys of the haw thorn clene gaderyd and bray hem al to duſt and temper hem wyth Almaunde mylk and aly yt wyth amydoñ and wyth eyryn wel þykke[t] and boyle it and meſſe yt forth and flowrys and levys abovȳ on[u].

[o] To be underſtood plurally, *Ears*.

[p] Miſwritten for *mycyd*, i. e. minced onyons.

[q] Vide N° 52.

[r] Stiffen, thicken it. See N° 44. where *lyed* has that ſenſe. See alſo 46.

[s] This diſh, no doubt, takes its name from *Spina*, of which it is made.

[t] Read, þykke, *thykke*.

[u] It means *laid upon it*.

XLVII. For to make Rofee [x] and Frefe [z] and Swan fchal be ymad in the felve maner.

Nym pyggus and hennys and other maner frefch flefch and hew yt in morfelys and feth yt in wyth wyn and [y] gyngyner and galyngale and gelofr' and canel [z] and bray yt wel and keft thereto and alye yt wyth amydoñ other wyth flowr of rys.

XLVIII. For to make an amendement Formete that ys to [a] falt and over mychyl.

Nym etemele and bynd yt in a fayr lynnen clowt and lat yt honge in the pot fo that yt thowche nozt the bottym and lat it hongy ther'ynne a god wyle and feþh [b] fet yt fro the fyre and let yt kele and yt fchal be frefch ynow wythoute any other maner li- cowr ydo ther'to.

XLIX. For to make Rapy [c].

Tak Fygys and reyfyns and wyn and grynd hem togeder tak and draw hem thorw a cloth and do ther'to powder of Alkenet other of rys and do ther'to a god quantite of pepir and vyneger and boyle it togeder and meffe yt and ferve yt forth.

[x] Vide N° 41.
[y] Perhaps, *in wyn with.*
[z] Cinamon. Vide Gloff.
[a] id eft, *too.*
[b] Read, *feth,* i. e. then.
[c] Vide Part II. N° 1. 28.

L. For

L. For to make an Egge Dows [d].

Tak Almaundys and mak god mylk and temper wyth god wyneger clene tak reyſynys and boyle hem in clene water and tak the reyſynis and tak hem owt of the water and boyle hem wyth mylk and zyf thow wyl colowr yt wyth ſafroñ and ſerve yt forth.

LI. For to make a mallard in cyney [e].

'Tak a mallard and pul hym drye and ſwyng over the fyre draw hym but lat hym touche no water and hew hym in gobettys and do hym in a pot of clene water boyle hem wel and tak onyons and boyle and bred and pepyr and grynd togedere and draw thorw a cloth temper wyth wyn and boyle yt and ſerve yt forth.

LII. For to make a Bukkenade [f].

Tak veel and boyle it tak zolkys of eggys and mak hem thykke tak macis and powdr' of gyngyn' and powder of peper and boyle yt togeder and meſſe yt forth.

---

[d] Vide ad Part II. N° 21. There are no eggs concerned, ſo no doubt it ſhould be *Eger Dows*. Vide Gloſſ.

[e] See N° 8.

[f] Vide N° 45.

LIII.

LIII. For to make a Roo Broth [g].

Tak Parſile and Yſop and Sauge and hak yt ſmal boil it in wyn and in water and a lytyl powdr' of peper and meſſe yt forth.

LIV. For to mak a Bruet of Sarcyneſſe.

Tak the lyre of the freſch Buf and bet it al iŋ pecis and bred and fry yt in freſch gres tak it up and and drye it and do yt in ꜹ veſſel wyth wyn and ſugur and powdr' of clowys boyle yt togedere tyl the fleſch have drong the liycour' and take the almande mylk and quibibz macis and clowys and boyle hem togeder' tak the fleſch and do the[r]'to and meſſe it forth.

LV. For to make a Gely [h].

Tak hoggys fet other pyggys other erys other par-trichys other chiconys and do hem togeder' and ſeɲh [i] hem in a pot and do hem in flowr' of canel and clowys other or grounde [k] do ther'to vineger and tak and do the broth in a clene veſſel of al thys and tak the Fleſch and kerf yt in ſmal morſelys and do yt therein

---

[g] *Deer* or *Roes* are not mentioned, as in Mr. Brander's Roll, N° 14, ergo quære. It is a meager buſineſs. Can it mean *Rue-Broth* for penitents?

[h] Jelly.

[i] ſeþ, i. e. *ſeeth*.

[k] Not clearly expreſſed. It means either Cinamon or Cloves, and either in flour or ground.

tak

tak powder of galyngale and caſt above and lat yͤ
kels tak bronches of the lorer tr' and ſtyk over it and
kep yt al ſo longe as thou wilt and ſerve yt forth.

LVI. For to kepe Veniſon fro reſtyng.

Tak veniſon wan yt ys newe and cuver it haſtely
wyth Fern that no wynd may come thereto and wan
thou haſt ycuver yt wel led yt hom and do yt in a
ſoler that ſonne ne wynd may come ther'to and di-
membr' it and do yt in a clene water and lef yt ther'
half a day and after do yt up on herdeles for to drie
and wan yt ys drye tak ſalt and do after thy veniſon
axit [1] and do yt boyle in water that yt be other [m] ſo
ſalt als water of the ſee and moche more and after
lat the water be cold that it be thynne and thanne
do thy Veniſon in the water and lat yt be therein
thre daies and thre nyzt [n] and after tak yt owt of the
water and ſalt it wyth drie ſalt ryzt wel in a barel
and wan thy barel ys ful cuver it haſtely that ſunne
ne wynd come thereto.

LVII. For to do away Reſtyn [o] of Veniſon.

Tak the Veniſon that ys reſt and do yt in cold
water and after mak an hole in the herthe and lat
yt be thereyn thre dayes and thre nyzt and after tak

---

[1] as thy veniſon requires.   See Gloſſ. to Chaucer for *axe*.
[m] Dele.
[n] A plural, as in N° 57.
[o] Reſtineſs.   It ſhould be rather *reſtyng*.   See below.

yt up and ſpot yt wel wyth gret ſalt of peite [p] there were the reſtyng ys and after lat yt hange in reyn water al nyzt or mor'.

LVIII. For to make pōn̄dorroge [q].

Tak Partrichis wit [r] longe filettis of Pork al raw and hak hem wel ſmale and bray hem in a morter and wan they be wel brayed do thereto god plente of pouder and zolkys of eyryn and after mak ther'of a Farſure formed of the gretneſſe of a onyon̄ and after do it boyle in god breth of Buf other of Pork after lat yt kele and after do it on a broche of Haſel and do them to the fere to roſte and after mak god bature of flour' and egg' on batur' wyt and another zelow and do thereto god plente of ſugur and tak a fethere or a ſtyk and tak of the batur' and peynte ther'on above the applyn ſo that on be wyt and that other zelow wel colourd.

Explicit ſerviciurn de carnibus.

[p] Pierre, or Petre.
[q] Vide N° 42.
[r] with.

Hic

Hic incipit Servicium de Pissibus[a].

I. For to make Egardufe[b].

TAK Lucys[c] or Tenchis and hak hem fmal in go-bett' and fry hem in oyle de olive and fyth nym vineger and the thredde party of fugur and myncyd onyons fmal and boyle al togeder' and caft ther'yn clowys macys and quibibz and ferve yt forthe.

II. For to make Rapy[d].

Tak pyg' or Tenchis or other maner frefch fyfch and fry yt wyth oyle de olive and fyth nym the cruftys of wyt bred and canel and bray yt al wel in a mortere and temper yt up wyth god wyn and cole[e] yt thorw an herfyve and that yt be al cole[f] of canel and boyle yt and caft ther'in hole clowys and macys

---

[a] See p. 1.

[b] See N° 21 below, and part I. N° 50.

[c] Lucy, I prefume, means the *Pike*; fo that this fifh was known here long before the reign of H. VIII. though it is commonly thought otherwife. V. Glofſ.

[d] Vide N° 49.

[e] Strain, from Lat. *colo*.

[f] Strained, or cleared.

P   and

and quibibz and do the fyfch in difchis and rape ᵍ
abovyn and dreffe yt forthe.

III. For to make Fygey.

Nym Lucys or tenchis and hak hem in morfell'
and fry hem tak vyneger and the thredde party of
fugur myncy onyons fmal and boyle al togedyr caft
ther'yn macis clowys quibibz and ferve yt forth.

IIII. For to make Pommys morles.

Nym Rys and bray hem ʰ wel and temper hem up
wyth almaunde mylk and boyle yt nym applyn and
par' hem and fher hem fmal als dicis and caft hem
ther'yn after the boylyng and caft fugur wyth al and
colowr yt wyth fafron and caft ther'to pouder and
ferve yt forthe.

V. For to make rys moyle ⁱ.

Nym rys and bray hem ryzt wel in a morter and
caft ther'to god Almaunde mylk and fugur and falt
boyle yt and ferve yt forth.

VI. For to make Sowpys dorry.

Nym onyons and mynce hem fmale and fry hem in

ᵍ This Rape is what the difh takes its name from. Perhaps
means *grape* from the French *raper*. Vide Nᵒ 28.

ʰ Rice, as it confifts of grains, is here confidered as a plural.
See alfo Nᵒ 5. 7, 8.

ⁱ Vide Gloff.

oyl

oyl dolyf Nym wyn and boyle yt wyth the onyouns
tofte wyte bred and do yt in difchis and god Almande
mylk alfo and do ther'above and ferve yt forthe.

VII. For to make Blomanger [k] of Fyfch.

Tak a pound of rys les hem wel and wafch and
feth tyl they brefte and lat hem kele and do ther'to
mylk of to pound of Almandys nym the Perche or the
Lopufter and boyle yt and keft fugur and falt alfo
ther'to and ferve yt forth.

VIII. For to make a Potage of Rys.

Tak Rys and les hem and wafch hem clene and
feth hem tyl they brefte and than lat hem kele and
feth caft ther'to Almand mylk and colour it wyth fafron and boyle it and meffe yt forth.

IX. For to make Lamprey frefch in Galentyne [l].

Schal be latyn blod atte Navel and fchald yt and
roft yt and ley yt al hole up on a Plater and zyf hym
forth wyth Galentyn that be mad of Galyngale gyngener and canel and dreffe yt forth.

X. For to make falt Lamprey in Galentyne [m].

Yt fchal be ftoppit [n] over nyzt in lews water and

---

[k] See note on N° 14. of Part I.

[l] This is a made or compounded thing. See both here, and in
the next Number, and v. Gloff.

[m] See note [l] on the laft Number.

[n] Perhaps, *ftppit*, i. e. fteeped. See N° 12.

in

in braan and flowe and ſodyn and pyl onyons and ſeth hem and ley hem al hol by the Lomprey and ȝif hem forthe wyth galentyne makyth [o] wyth ſtrong vyneger and wyth paryng of wyt bred and boyle it al togeder' and ſerve yt forthe.

XI. For to make Lampreys in Bruet.

They ſchulle be ſchaldyd and yſode and ybrulyd upon a gredern and grynd peper and ſafrō and do ther'to and boyle it and do the Lomprey ther'yn and ſerve yt forth.

XII. For to make a Storchō.

He ſchal be ſhorn in beſys [p] and ſtepyd [q] over nyȝt and ſodyn longe as Fleſch and he ſchal be etyn in venegar.

XIII. For to make Solys in Bruet.

They ſchal be fleyn and ſodyn and roſtyd upon a gredern and grynd Peper and Safrō and ale boyle it wel and do the ſole in a plater and the bruet above ſerve it forth.

XIV. For to make Oyſtryn in Bruet.

They ſchul be ſchallyd [r] and yſod in clene water

[o] Perhaps, *makyd*, i. e. made.
[p] Perhaps, *peſys*, i. e. pieces.
[q] Qu. *ſteppit*, i. e. ſteeped.
[r] Have ſhells taken off.

gryndicati

grynd peper ſafroñ bred and ale and temper it wyth
Broth do the Oyſtryn ther'ynne and boyle it and ſalt
it and ſerve it forth.

XV. For to make Elys in Bruet.

They ſchul be flayn and ket in gobett' and ſodyn
and grynd peper and ſafroñ other myntys and perſele
and bred and ale and temper it wyth the broth and
boyle it and ſerve it forth.

XVI. For to make a Lopiſter.

He ſchal be roſtyd in his ſcalys in a ovyn other by
the Feer under a panne and etyn wyth Veneger.

XVII. For to make Porreyne.

Tak Prunys fayriſt waſch hem wel and clene and
frot hem wel in ſyve for the Jus be wel ywronge and
do it in a pot and do ther'to wyt gres and a party of
ſugur other hony and mak hem to boyle togeder' and
mak yt thykke with flowr of rys other of waſtel bred
and wan it is ſodyn dreſſe it into diſchis and ſtrew
ther'on powder and ſerve it forth.

XVIII. For to make Chireſeye.

Tak Chiryes at the Feſt of Seynt John the Baptiſt
and do away the ſtonys grynd hem in a morter and
after frot hem wel in a ſeve ſo that the Jus be wel
comyn owt and do than in a pot and do ther'in feyr
gres

gres or Boter and bred of waſtrel ymyid ˢ and of
ſugur a god party and a porcion̄ of wyn and wan it
is wel yſodyn and ydreſſyd in Dyſchis ſtik ther'iɴ
clowis of Gilofr' and ſtrew ther'on ſugur.

XIX. For to make Blank de Sur' ᵗ.

Tak the zolkys of Eggs ſodyn and temper it wyth
mylk of a kow and do ther'to Comyn and Safron̄ and
flowr' of ris or waſtel bred mycd and grynd in a morter
and temper it up wyth the milk and mak it boyle
and do ther'to wit ᵘ of Egg' corvyn ſmale and tak fat
cheſe and kerf ther'to wan the licour is boylyd and
ſerve it forth.

XX. For to make Grave enforſe.

Tak tȳd ʷ gyngener and Safron̄ and grynd hem in
a morter and temper hem up wyth Almandys and do
hem to the fir' and wan it boylyth wel do ther'to
zolkys of Egg' ſodyn and fat cheſe corvyn in gobettis
and wan it is dreſſid in diſchis ſtrawe up on Powder of
Galyngale and ſerve it forth.

XXI. For to make Hony Douſe ˣ.

Tak god mylk of Almandys and rys and waſch
hem wel in a feyr' veſſel and in fayr' hoth water and

ˢ Perhaps, *ymycid*, i. e. minced ; or *mycd*, as in Nº 19.
ᵗ Vide Note ᶜ on Nº 29. of Part I.
ᵘ white. So *wyt* is *white* in Nº 2 L below.
ʷ It appears to me to be *tryd*. Can it be *fryd?*
ˣ See Part II. Nº 1 ; and Part I. Nº 50.

after

after do hem in a feyr towayl for to drie and wan
that they be drye bray hem wel in a morter al to
flowr' and afterward tak two partyis and do the half
in a pot and that other half in another pot and colowr that on wyth the fafron̄ and lat that other be
wyt and lat yt boyle tyl it be thykke and do ther'to
a god party of fugur and after dreffe yt in twe difchis
and loke that thou have Almandys boylid in water
and in fafron̄ and in wyn and after frie hem and fet
hem upon the fyre fethith mete ʸ and ſtrew ther'on
fugur that yt be wel ycolouryt ᶻ and ſerve yt forth.

XXII. For to make a Potage Feneboiles.

Tak wite benes and feth hem in water and bray
the benys in a morter al to nozt and lat them fethe
in almande mylk and do ther'in wyn and hony and
feth ᵃ reyfons in wyn and do ther'to and after dreffe
yt forth.

XXIII. For to make Tartys in Applis.

Tak gode Applys and gode Spycis and Figys and
reyfons and Perys and wan they are wel ybrayed colourd ᵇ wyth Safron̄ wel and do yt in a cofyn and do
yt forth to bake wel.

ʸ Seth it mete, i. e. feeth it properly.
ᶻ Coloured. See N° 28. below.
ᵃ i. e. Seeth.
ᵇ Perhaps, *coloure*.

XXIV.

XXIV. For to make Rys Alker'.

Tak Figys and Reyſons and do awey the Kernelis and a god party of Applys and do awey the paryng of the Applis and the Kernelis and bray hem wel in a morter and temper hem up with Almande mylk and menge hem wyth flowr of Rys that yt be wel chariaunt and ſtrew ther'upon powder of Galyngale and ſerve yt forth.

XXV. For to make Tartys of Fyſch owt of Lente.

Mak the Cowche of fat cheſe and gyngener and Canel and pur' crym of mylk of a Kow and of Helys yſodyn and grynd hem wel wyth Safrõ and mak the chowche of Canel and of Clowys and of Rys and of gode Spycys as other Tartys fallyth to be.

XXVI. For to make Morrey ᶜ.

Requir' de Carnibus ut ſupra ᵈ.

XXVII. For to make Flownys ᵉ in Lente.

Tak god Flowr and mak a Paſt and tak god mylk of Almandys and flowr of rys other amydõ and boyle hem togeder' that they be wel chariaud wan yt is boylid thykke take yt up and ley yt on a feyr'

ᶜ Vide Part I. Nº 37.

ᵈ Part I. Nº 37.

ᵉ Perhaps, *Flawnes*, or Cuſtards. Chaucer, vide *Slaunis*. Fr. *Flans*.

bord

bord fo that yt be cold and wan the Cofyns ben makyd tak a party of and do upon the coffyns and kerf hem in Schiveris and do hem in god mylk of Almandys and Figys and Datys and kerf yt in fowr partyis and do yt to bake and ferve yt forth.

XXVIII. For to make Rapee [f].

Tak the Cruftys of wyt bred and reyfons and bray hem wel in a morter and after temper hem up wyth wyn and wryng hem thorw a cloth and do ther'to Canel that yt be al colouryt of canel and do ther'to hole clowys macys and quibibz the fyfch fchal be Lucys other Tenchis fryid or other maner Fyfch fo that yt be frefch and wel yfryed and do yt in Difchis and that rape up on and ferve yt forth.

XXIX. For to make a Porrey Chapeleyn.

Tak an hundred onyons other an half and tak oyle de Olyf and boyle togeder' in a Pot and tak Almande mylk and boyle yt and do ther'to. Tak and make a thynne Paaft of Dow and make therof as it were ryngis tak and fry hem in oyle de Olyve or in wyte grees and boil al togedere.

XXX. For to make Formenty on a Fichfsday [g].

Tak the mylk of the Hafel Notis boyl the wete [h] wyth the aftermelk til it be dryyd and tak and colour[d] [i] yt wyth Safron and the ferft mylk caft ther'to and boyle wel and ferve yt forth.

[f] Vide Part I. N° 49. [g] Fifhday. [h] white. [i] Perhaps, *colour.*

Q

XXXI.

XXXI. For to make Blank de Syry [k].

Tak Almande mylk and Flowr' of Rys Tak ther'to ſugur and boyle thys togeder' and diſche yt and tak Almandys and wet hem in water of Sugur and drye hem in a panne and plante hem in the mete and ſerve yt forth.

XXXII. For to make a Pynade or Pyvade.

Take Hony and Rotys of Radich and grynd yt ſmal in a morter and do yt ther'to that hony a quantite of broun ſugur and do ther'to Tak Powder of Peper and Safroñ and Almandys and do al togeder' boyl hem long and hold[l] yt in a wet bord and let yt kele and meſſe yt and do yt forth [m].

XXXIII. For to make a Balourgly [n] Broth.

Tak Pikys and ſpred hem abord and Helys zif thou haſt fle hem and ket hem in gobettys and ſeth hem in alf wyn[o] and half in water Tak up the Pykys and Elys and hold hem hote and draw the Broth thorwe a Clothe do Powder of Gyngener Peper and Galyngale and Canel into the Broth and boyle yt and do yt on the Pykys and on the Elys and ſerve yt forth.

𝕰𝖗𝖕𝖑𝖎𝖈𝖎𝖙 𝖉𝖊 𝕮𝖔𝖖𝖚𝖎𝖓𝖆 𝖖𝖚𝖊 𝖊𝖘𝖙 𝖔𝖕𝖙𝖎𝖒𝖆 𝖒𝖊𝖉𝖎𝖈𝖎𝖓𝖆.

[k] Vide ad Nº 29. cf Part I.
[l] i. e. *keep*, as in next Number.
[m] This Recipe is ill expreſſed.
[n] This is ſo uncertain in the original, that I can only gueſs at it.
[o] Perhaps, *alf in wyr*, or dele *in* before *water*.

INDEX.

INDEX AND GLOSSARY

TO

MR. BRANDER'S ROLL OF COOKERY.

The Numbers relate to the order of the Recipes.

N. B. Many words are now written as one, which formerly were divided, as al fo, up on, &c. Of thefe little notice is taken in the Index, but I mention it here once for all.

Our orthography was very fluctuating and uncertain at this time, as appears from the different modes of fpelling the fame words. v. To gedre; v. wayfhe; v. ynowkz; v. chargeant; v. corānte; &c.

A.

A. abounds. a gode broth, 5. 26, al a nyzt, 192. *in.* a two, 62.

ā. and. paffim.

Aftir. Proem. like, 176. Wiclif.

Aray. Drefs, fet forth, 7. Chaucer.

Alf. MS. Ed. 45. II. 33. half.

Alye it. 7. 33. mix, thicken. hence *alloy* of metals. from French *allayer.* alay, 22. aly, MS. Ed. 46. See Junij Etymolog. v. Alaye. lye. here Nº 15.

lyed.

lyed. thickened. MS. Ed. 44, 45. Randle Holme interprets lyth or lything by thickening. hence lyō. a mixture, 11. *alith* for alyed. MS. Editor. N° 45.

Awey. MS. Ed. 27. II. 18. away.

Auance. 6. forte Avens. *Caryophylla*, Miller, Gard. Dict.

Axe. MS. Ed. N° 56. Chaucer.

Ayren. v. Eyren.

Al, Alle. 23. 53. Proem. All. Chaucer. *al to breſt.* all burſt. MS. Ed. N° 14.

Als. MS. Editor. N° 29. Chaucer. in v. It means *as.*

Almandes. 17. very variouſly written at this time, Almaunde, Almandys, Almaundys, Almondes, all which occur in MS. Ed. and mean Almond or Almonds.

Almand mylke. 9. Almonds blanch'd and drawn thickiſh with good broth or water, N° 51. is called *thyk mylke,* 52. and is called after Almande mylke, firſt and ſecond milk, 116. Almands unblanched, ground, and drawn with good broth, is called mylke, 62. Cow's milk was ſometimes uſed inſtead of it, as MS. Ed. 1. 13.

Creme of Almands, how made, 85. Of it, Lel. Coll. VI. p. 17. We hear elſewhere of Almond-butter, v. Butter.

Azeyn. 24. again. Lel. Coll. IV. p. 281. alibi. Chaucer. A. S. Aȝen.

Aneys, Anyſe. 36. 137. Aneys in confit rede other whyt, 36. 38. i. e. Anis or Aniſeed confectioned red, or white. uſed for garniſh, 58.

Amydon. 37. v. ad locum.

Almony. 47. v. ad locum.

Almayne. 71. Germany. v. ad loc. MS. Editor, N° 2. 31.

Alkenet. 47. A ſpecies of Buglos. Quincey, Diſpenſ. p. 51. 62. uſed for colouring, 51. 84. fryed and yfondred, or yfondyt, 62. 162.

Anoon.

Anoon. 53. Anon, immediately. Wiclif.

Arn. MS. Ed. II. 23. are. Chaucer. v. *arne.*

Adoñ. 59. 85. down. v. Chaucer. voce *advune.* MS.
Edit. Nº 1.

Avyfement. Proem. Advice, Direction. Chaucer.
French.

Aymers. 72. Embers. Sax. æmýpıan, Cineres. Belg.
ameren.

Aquapatys. 75. a Mefs or Difh.

Alker. Rys Alker. MS. Ed. II. 24.

Appulmoy. 79. a difh. v. ad loc. Appelyn, Applys,
Apples. MS. Ed. 17. 35.

Abrode. 85. abrod. MS. Ed. II. 33. abroad. So
brode. MS. Ed. 15. broad.

Alite. v. Lite.

Ale. 113. v. Pref.

Afide. 113. apart. Wiclif.

Ayfell. 114, 115. a fpecies of Vinegar. Wiclif.
Chaucer. v. *Eijel.*

Alegar. 114.

Armed. 146. v. ad loc.

Alygyn. v. Brewet.

B.

Bacon. Nº 1.

Benes. 1. alibi Beans. Chaucer. v. *bene.*

Bef. 6. MS. Ed. 17. Beef. Buf, Buff. MS. Ed. 27.
42, 43.

Buth. 6. 23. 30. alibi. been, are. Chaucer has *beth.*

Ben. MS. Ed. 4. 27. be. Chaucer v. *bein* and *ben.*

Balles. 152. Balls or Pellets.

Blank Defire. 193, 194. bis. Lel. Coll. VI. p. 5. In
Nº 193, we meet with *Blank defne,* but the Contents has *Defire,* which is right, as appears from
thē fequel. In MS. Ed. 29. it is *Blank-Surry,* and
Sury, and *Sure,* and *de Sur.* II. 19. de Syry, 31.

4   and

and here N° 37, it is Defforre. and we have *Samon in Sorry*. Lel. Coll. VI. p. 17. Perches. ibid. Eels p. 28. 30. where it is a Potage. whence I conceive it either means *de Surrey*, i. e. Syria. v. Chaucer. v. *Surrey*. Or it may mean *to be defired*, as we have *Horfys of Defyr*. Lel. Coll. IV. p. 272. See N° 63. and it is plainly written *Defire* in Godwin de Præful. p. 697. In this cafe, the others are all of them corruptions.

Blank Defforre. v. Blank Defire.

Blank Defne. v. Blank Defire.

Berandyles. MS. Ed. 27.

Bred, Breed. MS. Ed. paffim. Bread.

Bove. 167. Above. Chaucer. Belg. *Boven*.

Blode. 11. alibi. Blod. MS. Ed. 9. Blood.

Batō. 149. of eggs, 161. 179. Batur, 28. Batour. ibid. 19. Batter.

Boter. MS. Ed. 38. Butter.

Borage. 6.

Betes. 6. Beets. Fr. *Bete*.

Burfen. 11. name of a difh. Burfews, N° 179, is a different difh.

Brek. MS. Ed. 6. 23. break, bruife.

Breft, brefte. MS. Ed. 1. 14. burft.

Bukkennade. 17. a difh. Buknade, 118. where it means a mode of dreffing. vide MS. Ed. 45. 52.

Bryddes. 19. Briddes, 60. 62. Birds, per metathefin. Chaucer.

Brawn of Capons. 20. 84. Flefh. Braun. MS. Ed. 29. v. Chaucer. we now fay, *brawn of the arm*, meaning the flefh. Hence *brawn fall'n*. Old Plays, XI. p. 85. Lylie's Euphues, p. 94. 142. Chaucer. Brawn is now appropriated to thefe rolls which are made of Brawn or Boar, but it was not fo anciently, fince in N° 32 we have *Brawn of Swyne*, which fhews the word was common to other kinds

of

of flesh as well as that of the Boar; and therefore I cannot agree with Dr. Wallis in deducing *Brawn* from *Aprugna.*

Blank maṅg. 36. 192. Chaucer writes *Blank manger.* Blomanger. MS. Ed. 14. 33. 34. II. 7. N. B. a very different thing from what we make now under that name, and see Holme, III. p. 81.

Bronchis. MS. Ed. 55. Branches.

Braan. MS. Ed. II. 10. Bran.

Bet. MS. Ed. II. 21. Beaten.

Broche. MS. Ed. 58. a Spit.

Brewet of Almony. 47. v. Almony. of Ayrēn, or eggs, 91. MS. Ed. 23. Eles in Brewet, 110. where it feems to be compofed of Bread and Wine. Mufkles in Brewet, 122. Hens in Bruet, MS. Ed. 7. Cold, 131. 134. Bruet and Brewet are French *Brouet,* Pottage or Broth. Bruet riche, Lel. Coll. IV. p. 226. *Beorwcte,* p. 227, as I take it. *Blanche Brewct de Alyngyn,* MS. Ed. 13. 23.

Boon. 55. Bone. Chaucer.

Brenȳng. 67. 188. burning, per metathefin, from *bren* or *brenne,* ufed by Skelton, in the Invective againft Wolfey; and many old authors. Hence the difeafe called brenning or burning. Motte's Abridgement of Phil. Tranf. part IV. p. 245. Reid's Abridgement, part III. p. 149. Wiclif has *brenne* and *bryn.* Chaucer. v. *bren, Brinne,* &c.

Blake. 68. Black. Chaucer.

Berft. 70. 181. 192. burft. Chaucer. A. S. bepȷꞃꞇan.

Breth. 71. Air, Steam. MS. Ed. N° 2. hence *brethcr,* breather. Wiclif.

Broṅ. 74. brown. A. S. bꞃun.

Butter. 81. 91. 92. 160. Boter, MS. Ed. 38. and fo *boutry* is Buttery. Lel. Coll. IV. p. 281. *Almonde Butter.* Lel. VI. p. 6. Rabelais, IV. c. 60.

Bynethen. 92. under, beneath. Chaucer. bineth.

Bolas. 95. bullace. Chaucer.

Bifore.

Bifore. 102. before. Wiclif. Matth. xiv. Chaucer has *biforne*, and byforne.

Brafey. a compound fauce, 107.

Ballac broth. 109.

Brymlent. Tart de Brymlent. 167. v. ad loc.

Bloms. 171. Flowers, Bloſſoms. Chaucer.

Bothom. 173. bottom. pronounced *bothom* now in the north. Chaucer. bottym, MS. Ed. 48.

Brode. 189. broad. v. abrode.

Bataiwyng. 189. embatteling. qu. if not miſread for *bataillyng*. See Chaucer. v. batailed.

Bord. MS. Ed. II. 27. board. Chaucer.

Breyt, breth. MS. Ed. 17. 58. Broth.

Blank Surry. MS. Ed. 29. II. 19. v. Blank Deſire.

Biſmeus. MS. Ed. 16.

C.

C. omitted. v. Cok. v. pluk. v. Pryk. v. Pekok. v. Phiſik. v. thyk. on the contrary it often abounds, hence, ſchulle, ſhould ; freſch, freſh ; diſche, diſh ; ſchepys, ſheeps ; fleſch, fleſh ; fyſch, fiſh ; ſcher, cheer, &c. in MS. Ed. v. Gl. to Chaucer. v. ſchal.

Craftly. Proem. properly, *ſecundum artem.*

Caboches. 4. alibi. Cabbages. f. Fr. Caboche, Head, Pate.

Caraway. 53. v. Junij Etymolog.

Carvon. 152. carved, cut. Corvyn, MS. Ed. II. 19, 20. cut. *Corue*, i. e. corve, 4. cut. v. ycorve. v. kerve.

Canell. paſſim. Cinamon. Wiclif. v. Pref.

Cuver. MS. Ed. 56. Cover.

Cumpas. by Cumpas, i. e. Compaſs, 189. by meaſure, or round. Lel. Coll. IV. p. 263.

Cool. 6. Cole or Colwort. Belg. *kool.*

Corat. 12. name of a diſh.

Culdore. MS. Ed. 25. 27. a Cullender. Span. Coladers.

Caſſelys. MS. Ed. 28.

Cranes.

Cranes. 146. *Grues.* v. ad loc.

Chyballes. 12. Chibolls, 76. young Onions. Littleton. Ital. *Cibolo.* Lat. Cæpula, according to Menage; and fee Lye.

Colys. MS. Ed. II. fee the Pref.

Cawdel. 15. 33. Caudell, Contents. See Junius. of Muſkels or Muſcles, 124. Cawdel Ferry, 41. In E. of Devon's feaſt it is *Feny.*

Conynges. 17. Connynges, 25. Coneys, Rabbets.

Calle. 152. Cawl of a Swine.

Connat. 18. a marmolade. v. ad loc.

Clowes. 20. Cloves. v. Pref.

Canuas, or Canvaſs. 178. Fr. Canevas. Belg. Kaneſas.

Corañte. Rayſoñs of Corañte. 14. So *Rafyns of Corens,* Northumb. Book, p. 19. *Raiſin de Corintiie.* Fr. i. e. of Corinth, whence our Currants, which are ſmall Raiſins, came, and took their name. *Corance,* 17. 21. *Coraunce,* 50. *Coronſe,* MS. Ed. 42. Raiſins are called by way of contradiſtinction *grete* Rayſoñs, 65. 133. See Northumb. Book, p. 11.

Coronſe. v. Corañte.

Chargeant. 192. Stiff. v. ad loc. MS. Ed. writes *Charchant,* 29, 30 *Charghaunt,* 33. *Charchaunt,* 34. *Chariaunt.* i. e. *Charjaunt,* 36. II. 24. *Chariand.* i. e. *Charjand,* 27.

Comyn. MS. Ed. 39.

Colure. MS. Ed. 5. to colour.

Concys. 22. feems to be a kind of ſauce. MS. Ed. 6. but the recipe there is different. v. ad N° 25.

Chanke. MS. Ed. 20.

Col, Cole. 23. 52. cool. alſo to ſtrain, 70, 71. alibi. MS. Ed. II. 22. cleared.

Comyn. MS. Ed. II. 18. come.

Cowche. 24. 154. lay. MS. Ed. II. 25. Chaucer, v. Couche.

Cyneé. 25. a certain ſauce. perhaps the ſame with Concy. N° 22. Plays in Cynee, 112. Sooles, 119. Tenches, 120. Oyſters, 123.

R
Harys

Harys [Hares] in Cmee. MS. Ed. 8. where
doubtlefs we fhould read Cinee, fince in N° 51
there it is *Cyney*. It is much the fame as *bruet*,
for *Sooles in Cynee* here is much the fame with
Solys in bruet. MS. Ed. II. 13.

Chykens. 27. 33. Chicken is a plural itfelf. but in
MS. Ed. 13. it is *Chekenys* alfo ; and *Chyckyns*. Lel.
Coll. IV. p. 1. *Checonys* MS. Ed.

Carnel of Pork. 32. v. ad loc.

Corvyn. v. Carvon.

Curlews. 35. not eaten now at good tables; however
they occur in archb. Nevill's feaft. Lel. Coll. VI.
p. 1. And fee Northumb. Book, p. 106. Rabelais
iv. c. 59. And Earl of Devon's Feaft.

Confit, or Confyt. v. Aneys and Colyandre.

Charlet. 39. a difh. v. ad loc.

Chefe ruayn. 49. 166. perhaps of Rouen in Nor-
mandy. *rouen* in Fr. fignifies the colour we call
roan.

Crems. 52. for fingular Cream. written *Creme*, 85.
183. Crem and Crym, in MS. Ed. 34. II. 24. Fr.
Crefme, Creme.

Cormarye. 53. a difh. qu.

Colyandre. 53. 128. where it is *in Confyt rede*, or
red. White is alfo ufed for garnifh, 59. Celenɔpe,
A. S. Ciliandro, Span.

Chyryfe. 58. a made difh of cherries. v. ad loc.

Cheweryes. 58. Cherries. v. ad loc. and MS. Ed. II.
18. ubi *Chiryes*.

Crotoñ, 60. a difh. v. ad loc.

Crayton. v. Crotoñ.

Cleeve a two. 62. cloven. A. S. cleoʀan.

Cyrip. 64. Sirrup. v. ad loc.

Chyches. 72. Vetches, v. ad loc.

Chawf. 74. warm. Fr. *Echauffer*, whence Chaucer
has *Efchaufe*.

Clat.

Clat. 78. a diſh. qu.

Chef. Proem. chief. Fr.

Calwar Salmōn. 98. v. ad loc.

Compoſt. 1co. a preparation ſuppoſed to be always at hand. v. ad loc.

Comfery. 190. Comfrey. v. ad loc.

Chargeours. 101. diſhes. v. ad 126.

Chyſanne. 103. to be eaten cold.

Congur. 104. 115. Lel. Coll. VI. p. 6. bis. p. 16. *Cungeri* are among the fiſh in Mr. Topham's MS. for the Conger, little uſed now, ſee Pennant. III. p. 115.

Coffyns. 113. Pies raiſed without their lids, 158. 167. 185. 196. MS. Ed. II. 23. 27. In Wiclif it denotes baſkets.

Comade. 113. Comadore. 188.

Coūtour. 113. Coverture, Lid of a Pye.

Codlyng. 94. grete Codelyng, 114. v. ad loc.

Chawdōn. 115. for Swans, 143. *Swan with Chawdron.* Lel. Coll. IV. p. 226. which I ſuppoſe may be true orthography. So *Swann with Chaudron.* Earl of Devon's Feaſt. And it appears from a MS. of Mr. Aſtle's, where we have among *Sawces*, *Swanne is good with Chaldron*, that *Chaldron* is a ſauce.

Crome. 131. Pulp, Kernel. Crūmes. 159. Chaucer. The Crum is now the ſoft part of a loaf, oppoſed to the cruſt.

Cury. Proem. Cookery. We have aſſumed it in the title.

Camelyne. 144. a ſauce. an *Canelyne*, from the flour of Canel?

Crudds. 150. 171. Curds, per metatheſin, as common in the north.

Cruſtards. 154. Pies, from the *Cruſt*. quære if our *Cuſtard* be not a corruption of Cruſtard ; Junius gives a different etymon, but whether a better, the Reader muſt judge. Cruſtard of fiſh, 156. of herbs,

R 2

157.

157. and in the Earl of Devon's Feaſt we have *un Paſte Cruſtade.*

Cryſpes. 162. Cryſpels. 163. v. ad loc. *Fritter Criſ-payne,* Lel. Coll. VI. p. 5. which in Godwin de Præful p. 697. is *Fruter Criſpin.*

Chawfō. 162. Cowfer, 173. a Chafing-diſh. Chafer. Lel. Coll. IV. p. 302. v. Junius voce *Chafe.*

Curoſe. 171. curiouſly. perhaps from *cure,* to cook. Chaucer has *corcuſe,* curious.

Clarry. 172. Clary.

Cotagres. 175. a diſh. v. ad loc.

Cok. 175. a Cock. ſic, Lel. Coll. IV. p. 227.

Chewets. 185. 186. a diſh. Rand. Holme, III. p. 78. 81, 82. Birch, Life of Prince Henry, p. 458.

Comadore. v. Comade.

Chaſtlet. 189. v. ad loc.

Chriſten. Proem. Chriſtian.

D.

Do. 1, 2. put, cauſe. MS. Ed. 2. 12. Chaucer. *make.* 56. dene, 48. So Chaucer has *do* for *done.*

Dof. do off. 101.

Draw. drawen 2. ſtrained. hence 3. 20. 23. *drawe the grewel thurgh a ſtraynour.*

To boil. 2. 17. as, *drawe hem up with gode brothe.* alſo 51. 74.

To put, 14. 41.

To make. 28. 47. as, *draw an Almande mylke.*

Dee. 152. ſingular of Dice, the Fr. Dè. v. quare.

Drepee. 19. a diſh. qu.

Dates. 20. 52. 158. the fruit.

Dyſsh. 24. diſh.

Deſſorre. 37. v. Blank deſire.

Douſt. 45. alibi Duſt.

Dowhz,

Dowhz. 50. Dowh. 92. Dow. MS. Ed. II. 29.
Dough, Paſte. A. S. bah.
Douce Ame. 63. quaſi a delicious diſh. v. Blank Deſire.
Drope. 67. drop. to baſte. MS. Ed. 28.
Dorry. Sowpes dorry, 82. Sops endorſed. from *endore,*
187. MS. Ed. 42. II. 6. vide ad 174.
Deel. 113. 170. part, ſome. v. Sum. Chaucer.
Dicayn. 172. v. ad loc.
Dokks, as *Sowre Dokks,* 173. Docks.
Dorryle. v. Pome.
Daryols. 183. a diſh. A Cuſtard baked in a Cruſt.
Hear Junius, v. Dairie. ' G. *dariole* dicitur libi
' genus, quod iiſdem Gallis alias nuncupatur *laic-*
' *teron* vel *flan de laict.*'
Deſne. v. Blank Deſire.
Deſire. v. Blank.
Dreſſit. 194. dreſſed. dreſſe. MS. Ed. 15. et paſſim.
Chaucer in voce. hence ydreſſy. MS. Ed. II. 18.
Dyſis. MS. Ed. 15. dice. v. quare.
Demembre, dimembre. MS. Ed. 31. diſmember.
Dows, douze. MS. Ed. 50. II. 21.
Drong. MS. Ed. 54. drunk.

E.

E. with *e* final after the conſonant, for *ea,* as brede,
bread ; benes, beans ; bete, beat ; breke, break ;
creme, cream ; clere, clear ; clene, clean ; mede,
mead ; mete, meat ; ſtede, ſtead ; whete, wheat ;
&c.
E with *e* final after the conſonant, for *ee,* as betes,
beets ; cheſe, cheeſe ; depe, deep ; fete, feet ;
grene, green ; nede, needful ; ſwete, ſweet.
Endorre. MS. Ed. 42. endorſe.
Ete. 103. eat. *cten,* 146. eaten. *etyn.* MS. Ed. 3. A. S.
etan. MS. Ed. 48. oat.

Enforſe.

Enforfe. MS. Ed. II. 20. feafoned.

Erbes. 7 herbs; *herbes*, 63. *erbys*, 151. Eerbis, 157.

Eyren, and Ayren. 7, 8. 15. Eyryn, MS. Ed. 1. Eggs.
' a merchant at the N. Foreland in Kent afked for
' eggs, and the good wyf anfwerede, that fhe coude
' fpeak no Frenfhe — another fayd, that he wolde
' have *eyren*, then the good wyf fayd that fhe un-
' derftood hym wel.' Caxton's Virgil, in Lewis'
Life of Caxton, p. 61. who notes ' See Sewel's
' Dictionary, v. *Ey*.' add, Urry's Chaucer. v. Aye
and Eye. Note here the old plural *en*, that *eggs* is
fometimes ufed in our Roll, and that in Wiclif *eye*,
or *ey* is the fingular, and in the *Germ*. See Chaucer.
v. *Aie*, and *Ay*.

Eowts. 6. v. ad loc.

Egurdouce. 21. v. ad loc. of Fyfshe, 133. Egge dows,
MS. Ed. 50. malè. Egerdufe. ibid. II. 1. Our N°
58, is really an Eagerdouce, but different from this
here. A Seville Orange is Aigre-douce. Cotgrave.

Efy. 67. eafy. efelich, 113. eafily. Chaucer.

Eny. 74. 173. any.

Elena Campana. 78. i. e. Enula Campana, *Elecampane*.

Erbowle. 95. a difh. v. ad loc.

Erbolat. 172. a difh. v. ad loc.

Eerys, Eris. 177. 182. 55. Ears. *Eyr*. MS. Ed. 44.
Chaucer has *Ere* and *Eris*.

Elren. 171. Elder. *Eller*, in the north, without *d*.

Erne. 174. qu.

Euarund. MS. Fd. 3.

Eelys. 101. Eels. *Elys*, *Helys*. MS. Ed. II. 15. 24.
Elis Chaucer.

F.

Forced. 3. farced, ftuft. we now fay, *forc'd-meat*,
yfarced, 159, 160. *enforfed*. MS. Ed. II. 20. *fors*,
170.

170. called *fars*, 150. it feems to mean *feafon*, Nº 4.

Mixt. 4. where potage is faid to be *forced* with powdō-douce.

Fort. paffim. ftrong. Chaucer.

Frefee. MS. Ed. 47.

Fenkel. 6. 77. *Fenel*, 76. 172. *Fenell*, 100. Fennel. Germ. Venikol. Belg. Venckel.

Fome. Proem. 95. forme.

Funges. 10. Mufhrooms, from the French. Cotgrave. Holme III. p. 82. The Romans were fond of them.

Fefants. 20. 35.

Fynelich wel. 192. very wel, conftantly.

Fro. 22. MS. Ed. 5ʰ. Chaucer. from. So therfro. 53. Lel. Coll. IV. p. 266. Chaucer.

Fleyfch. 24. Fleifsh, 37. Flefh, A. S. ꝼlæꞃc. Germ. *Fleifc*.

Feneboyles. MS. Ed. II. 22.

Fyletts. 28. Fillets.

Florifh and Flō. 36. 38. 40. Garnifh. Lel. Coll. VI. p. 17. 23. Chaucer. v. Floure.

Foyles. 49. rolled Pafte. *Foyle of dowhz*, 50. 92. et per fe, 148. 153. *Foile of Pafte*, 163. Leaves of Sage, 161. Chaucer. v. ad 175. hence Carpe in Foile. Lel. Coll. IV. p. 226. *a Dolphin in Foyle, a futtletie.* VI. p. 5. *Lyng in Foyle*, p. 16. *Cunger.* Ibid. *Samon.* Ibid. *Sturgen.* p. 17. et v. p. 22. N. B. Foyle in thefe cafes means Pafte.

Fars. v. forced.

Fle. 53. flea, flaw. MS. Ed. II. 33. flawe, flein, flain, flawed. 10. 13. 15.

Fonnell. 62. a, difh.

Frot. MS. Ed. II. 17. rub, fhake, *frote*, Chaucer.

Feyre. 66. MS. Ed. II. 18. 22. *Feir.* Chaucer. Fair.

Ferthe. 68. Fourth. hence Ferthing or Farthing.

Furmente. 69. 116. *Furmenty.* MS. Ed. 1. *Formete.* Ibid. 48. *Formenty*, Ib. II. 30. from Lat. *Frumentum*,

tum, per metathefin; whence called more plaufibly *Frumity* in the north, and Frumetye in Lel. Collect. IV. p. 226. VI. p. 5. 17. 22. but fee Junius, v. Formetie.

Frenche. 73. a. difh. v. ad loc.

Feft. MS. II. 18. Feaft. Chaucer.

Fygey. 89. becaufe made of Figs. Fygs drawen. 103. MS. Ed. II. 3.

Found. 93. mix. diffolve, 193. fond. 188. v. y fonded. Lye, in Junii Etym. v. Founder.

Fcte. 102. Chaucer. Fet, MS. Ed. 44. Feet.

Flaumpeyns. 113. 184.

Ferft. MS. Ed. II. 30. Firft.

Fanne. 116. to fan or winnow. A. S. ꝼann, Vannus.

Frytō. 149, 150, 151. Fruturs. MS. Ed. 19. 4d. Fritters. *Fruter,* Lel. Coll. IV. p. 227. Frytor. VI. p. 17.

Flaunne. 163. Flownys. MS. Ed. II. 27. Fr. Flans, Cuftards. Chaucer. v. Slaunnis. Et v. Junium voce *Flawn.*

Feel. 168. hold, contain. perhaps fame as *feal,* occultare, abfcondere, for which fee Junii Etymol.

Fuyr. 188. Fire. *Fyr fort.* 192. a ftrong Fire. *Feré,* Chaucer. *Fyer,* Lel. Coll. IV. p. 296. Belg. *Vuyr. Fere.* MS. Ed. 58.

Ferry. v. Cawdel.

Flowr, Flowre. MS. Ed. 2. 19. Flour.

Fronchemoyle. MS. Ed. 15.

Froys. MS. Ed. 18. Fraife.

Farfure. MS. Ed. 28. ftuffing.

Forfy. MS. Ed. 38. feafon.

G.

Gronden. 1. 53. ground or beaten. *to grynde* is to cut or beat fmall. 3. 8. 13. for compare 14. ygrōnd 37. 53. 105. to pound or beat in a mortar. 3. MS. Ed. 5.

Gode.

Gode. N° 1. alibi. good, ſtrong. Chaucer. *god*, MS. Ed. paſſim.

Grete. mynced. 2. not too ſmall. *gretuſt*, 189. greateſt. *gret*, MS. Ed. 15. and Chaucer.

Gourdes. 8. Fr. gouhourde.

Gobettes. 16. 62. Gobbettys, Gobettis. MS. Ed. 9. alibi. Chaucer. *Gobbins*, Holme III. p. 81, 82. large pieces. Wiclif. Junii Etym.

Grees. 17. 101. Grece, 18. alibi. MS. Ed. 8. 14. 32. alibi. whyte Grece, 18. Fat, Lard, Conys of high Grece. Lel. Coll. IV. p. 226. qu.

Gravey. 26, 27. *Grave*. MS. Ed. II. 20. *Gravy*. Lel. Coll. VI. p. 10.

Galyntyne. 28. 117. a preparation ſeemingly made of ·Galingale, &c. 129. and thence to take its name. See a recipe for making it, 138. as alſo in MS. Ed. 9. Bread of Galyntyne, 94. Soupes of Galyntyne, 129. Lampervey in Galantine. Lel. Coll. IV. p. 226. VI. p. 22. Swanne, VI. p. 5.

Garlete and Garlec. 30. 34. Garlick. A. S. ʒaɲleac.

Grapes. 30. 34.

Galyngale. 30. the Powder, 47. the long-rooted Cy-perus. Gl. to Chaucer. See Northumberland Book, p. 415.

Gleyr̄. of Ayrēn. 59. the white, from Fr. glaire. Chaucer. *Lear* or *Leir* of an Egg. Holme inter-prets it *the White beaten into a foam*.

Goon. 59. MS. Ed. 1. go. Bel·g. *gaen*.

Gylofre. 65. Gelofre. MS. Ed. 27. cloves; for ſee N° 30, 31. 40. there; from Gr. *καρυόφυλλον*.

Gyngawdry. 94. a diſh.

Grave. MS. Ed. II. 20. Gravey.

Gele. 101, 102. Jelly. Fr. Gelée.

Gawdy Grene. 112. perhaps, Light Green.

Gurnards. 115.

Greynes de Parys. 137. and ſo Chaucer, meaning *Greynes de paradys*, or greater Cardamoms. See Dr.

S   Per**cy**

Percy on Northumb. Book, p. 414. Chaucer has *Greines* for *Grains.* and Belg. Greyn.

Grate. 152. v. i or y grated.

Gaftbon. 194. f. *Gaftbon,* quafi *Waftbon,* from *Waftel* the fineft Bread, which fee. Hence the Fr. Gafteau.

Gyngynyr, Gyngenyr, Gyngyner, Gyngener. MS. Ed. 3, 4. 13. 24. Ginger. Gyngyner-bred, 32.

Grotys. MS. Ed. II. Oat-meal Grotes, i. e. Grits.

Grydern, Gryder, Gredern. MS. Ed. 25. 44. II. 11.

H.

H. for *th,* as hem, them ; her, their; paffim. *Hare,* 121. Chaucer. Wiclif. It is fometimes omitted ; as *wyt* and *wyte,* white. Sometimes abounds, as fchaldyd. MS. Ed. 7. 11. fcalded. v. *Thowehe.*

Hye. Proem. high. *hy,* MS. Ed. 44. A. S. Heah.

Hē. 1, 2. i. e. hem ; them. Lye in Junii Etym.

Hulle. 1. a verb, to take off the hufk or fkin. Littleton. Hence Hulkes, Hufks or *Hulls,* as 71. *Holys,* MS. Ed. 1. Sax. helan, to cover. v. Lye in Junii Etym. v. Hull.

Hulkes. v. Hulle.

Hewe. 7. cut, mince. *yhewe,* 12. minced. hewn. MS. Ed. 6. 9. *hewin,* Chaucer. A. S. hepyan.

Hakke. 194. MS. Ed. 23. hack, bruife. Junii Etym. v. hack. MS. Ed. has alfo *hak* and *hac.*

Hebolace. 7. name of a dilh.

Herdeles. MS. Ed. 56. Hurdles.

Hennes. 17. 45. including, I prefume, the whole fpecies, as *Malard* and *Pekok* do below.

Hool. 20. 22. alibi. *hole,* 33. 175. *hoole,* 158. whole. Chaucer has hole, hool, and hoolich ; and Wiclif, *hole* and *hool.* MS. Ed. has *hol* and *hole.*

Hooles. 162. Holes.

Holfomly.

Holfomly. Proem. wholefomely.

Herthe. MS. Ed. 57. Earth.

Hit. 20. 98. 152. it. hytt. Northumb. Book, p. 440.
Hit, Gloff. Wiclif. in Marg. A. S. hıτ.

Hoot. 21. alibi. hot.

Hares. 23.

Hoggepot. 31. v. ad loc.

Hochee. 34. hachè, Fr. but there is nothing to intimate cutting them to pieces.

Herfyve. MS. Ed. II. 2. Hair-fieve. *her* is *hair* in Chaucer.

Helde. 50. 154. throw, caft, put. v. 189. *Heelde*, poured, fhed. Wiclif. and Lye in Junii Etym. v. Held.

Holde. 189. make, keep. MS. Ed. II. 32, 33.

Hawtheen. 57. Hawthorn. Junius, v. Haw.

Hatte. 59. bubling, wallop. quafi *the hot*, as in Chaucer. from A. Sax. haττ.

Hong. 67. hing, or hang. Chaucer. MS. Ed. 48.

Honde. 76. hand. Chaucer. So in Derbyfhire now.

Heps. 84. Fruit of the Canker-rofe. So now in Derbyfhire, and v. Junius, voce *Hippes*.

Hake. 94. 186. a Fifh. v. ad loc.

Hilde. 109. to fkin, from to hull. to fcale a fifh, 119. vide 117. 119. compared with MS. Ed. II. 13.

Herons. 146. MS. Ed. 3. Holme, III. p. 77, 78. but little ufed now. Heronfew. Lel. Coll. IV. p. 226. *Heronfhawe*. VI. p. 1. Heronfews. Chaucer. The Poulterer was to have in his fhop *Ardeas five airones,* according to Mr. Topham's MS. written about 1250. And *Heronns* appear at E. of Devon's Feaft.

Holke. 173. qu. hollow.

Hertrowee. 176. a difh. *Hert* is *the Hart* in Chaucer. A. S. heoɲτ.

Hi. MS. Ed. 27. they.

Hevyd. MS. Ed. 21. v. ad loc.

Hom. MS. Ed. 56. Home.

I.

I.

I. 2. for e. Proem. So *ith* for *eth*. Ibid.
I. 30. et fæpius. in. *inne*, 37. alibi.
Jufhell. 43. a difh. v. ad loc.
Is. plur. for es. 52. 73. Proem. Nomblys. MS. Ed.
  12. Nombles. v. Pees. Rofys, 177, Rofes.
I. for y. v. y.
Iowtes. v. Eowtes.
Irne. 107. *Iren*, Chaucer. and the Saxon. Iron.
Juys. 118. 131. *Jus*, MS. Ed. II. 17. the Fr. word.
  Ieufe, Chaucer.

K.

Kerve. 8. cut. *kerf*, 65. MS Ed. 29. v. carvon, and
  Chaucer, voc. Carfe, karft, kerve, kerft.
Kydde. 21. Flefh of a Kid. Kedys. MS. Ed. 13. Kids.
Keel. 29. 167. 188. MS. Ed. 1. Gl. to Chaucer and
  Wiclif, to cool.
Kyt. 118. alibi. MS. Ed. 19. *ket*, Ibid. II. 15. to cut.
  kyted, cut. Lel. Coll. IV. p. 298. Chaucer. v. *Kitt*.
Keintlick. v. queintlick.
Kyrnels. 189. a fpecies of battlements, from *kernellare*;
  for which fee Spelman, Du Frefne, and Chaucer.
Kever. MS. Ed. 2. cover.
Kafte, keft. MS. Ed. 6. 10. caft. v. ad loc.
Kow. MS. Ed. 38. Cow.

L.

L. for ll. MS. Ed. fæpe.
Lat. 9. 14. alibi. MS. Ed. 1, 2. Let. Chaucer. Belg.
  laten. latyn. MS. Ed. II. 9. *let.*

Lire,

Lire, and Lyre. 3. 14. 45. MS. Ed. fæpe. the flefhy part of Meat. A. S. lipe. See Lyre in Junii Etymol. Alfo a mixture, as *Dough of Bread and raw Eggs*, 15. hence '·drawe a Lyre of Brede, ' Blode, Vyneg, and Broth,' 25. So Lyō and Layō..11. 31. all from *lye*, which fee. Lay feems to mean *mix*, 31. as *layour* is mixture, 94.

Lye it up. 15. to mix; as *alye*, which fee.

Leke. in fing. 10. 76. Leeks.

Langdebef. 6. an herb. v. ad loc. *Longdobeef* Northumberland Book. p. 384. Buglofs.

Lytel. 19. paffim. *Litul* and *litull*, 104. 152. ' a litel ' of Vynegar,' 118. of Lard, 152.

Lofeyns, Lofyns. 24. 92. on fifh-day, 128. a Lozenge is interpreted by Cotgrave, ' a little fquare Cake of preferved herbs, flowers, &c.' but that feems to have no concern here. *Lozengs*. Lel. Coll. IV. p. 227.

Lyche. 152. like. *lichi*. Wiclif. *lich*. Chaucer. *ylich*. Idem.

Lombe. 62. Lamb. hence Wiclif, *Lomberen*, Lambs. Chaucer, and Germ.

Leche Lumbard. 65. from the country doubtlefs, as the muftard, N° 100. See alfo Lel. Coll. VI. p. 6. 26. *Leches*. MS. Ed. 15. are Cakes, or pieces. Rand. Holme makes *Leach*, p. 83. to be ' a kind ' of Jelly made of Cream, Ifing-glafs, Sugar, and ' Almonds, &c.' The *Leſſches* are fried, 158. v. yleefhyd. *Leyſe Damaſk*. Lel. Coll. IV. p. 226. *Leche baked*. VI. p. 5. *Partriche Leiche*. Ibid. *Leche Damaſke*. Ibid. See alfo, p. 10. *Leche Florentine*, p. 17. *Leche Comfort*. Ibid. *Leche Gramor*. Ibid. Leche Cypres, p. 26. which in Godwin de Præful. p. 697. is *Sipers*, malè.

Lete Lardes. 68. v. ad loc.

Lave. 76. wafh.

Leyne. 82. a Layer.

Lewe

Lewe water. 98. Lews water, MS. Ed. II. 10. warm;
   fee Glofſ. to Wiclif. and Junius. v. Lukewarm.

Lumbard Muſtard. 100. from the country. v. Leche,
   how made, Nº 145.

Lef. MS. Ed. 56. leave. *Lefe,* Chaucer.

Lite. 104. a few, *alite,* as they ſpeak in the North.
   Chaucer, v. Lite. and Lyte, and Mr. Lye in his
   Junius.

Laumpreys. 126. Lampreys. an Eel-like Sea Fiſh.
   Pennant, Brit. Zool. III. p. 68.

Laumprons. 127. the *Pride.* 'Pennant, Ibid. p. 61.
   See Lel. Coll. VI. p. 6. 17. bis 23. Mr. Topham's
   MS. has *Murenulas ſive Lampridulas.*

Looches, Loches. 130. 133. the fiſh.

Lardes of Swyne. 146. i. e. of Bacon. hence *lardid,*
   147. and *Lardons.* MS. Ed. 3. 43. from the Fr.
   which Cotgrave explains *Slices of Lard,* i. e. Bacon.
   vide ad 68.

Lorer tr̄. MS. Ed. 55. Laurel tree. Chaucer.

Lyuōs. 152. Livers. A. S. lẏꝼeꞃ.

Led. MS. Ed. 56. carry. *lide,* Chaucer.

Lenton. 158. Lent.

Lynḡ. 159. longer. Chaucer has *lenger* and *lengir.*
   v. Lange.

Lopuſter, Lopiſter. MS. Ed. II. 7. 16. v. Junii
   Etymolog.

Luſt. as, hym luſt. Proem. he likes. Chaucer. v. Leſt.

Lewys. MS. Ed. 41. Leaves. Lefe, Chaucer. v. Lef.

Lie. Liquor. Chaucer. MS. Ed. 48.

Ley. MS. Ed. 6. lay.

Leſe, les. MS. Ed. 14. II. 7, 8. pick. To *leaſe,* in Kent,
   is to glean.

M.

Make. 7. MS. Ed. 12. 43. II. 12. to dreſs. *make forth,*
   102. to do. MS. Ed. II. 35.

                                    Monchelet.

Monchelet. 16. a dish.

Mylk, Melk. MS. II. 30. Milk of Almonds, 1. 10. 13. alibi.

Moton. 16. MS. Ed. 1. Mutton. See Lel. Coll. IV. p. 226. Flemish. *Motoen.*

Mawmenee. 20. 193. a dish. v. ad loc. how made, 194. *Mamane.* Lel. Coll. IV. p. 227. Mamonie. VI. p. 17. 22. royal, 29. Manmene. MS. Ed. 29, 30. *Mamenge.* E. of Devon's Feast.

Morterelys. v. Mortrews.

Medle. 20. 50. alibi. to mix. Wiclif. Chaucer.

Messe. to messe the dysshes, 22. messe forth, 24.

Morre. 38. MS. Ed. 37. II. 26. a dish. v. ad loc.

Mortrews. 45. *Mortrews blank*, 46. of fish, 125. *Mor-terelys*, MS. Ed. 5. where the recipe is much the same. ' meat made of boiled hens, crummed bread, ' yolk of eggs, and safron, all boiled together,' Speght ad Chaucer. So called, says Skinner, who writes it *mortrefs*, because the ingredients are all pounded together in a mortar.

Moscels. 47. Morsels. Chaucer has *Morcills*. Moscels is not amiss, as *Mossil* in Chaucer is the muzle or mouth.

Mete. 67. A. S. and Chaucer. Meat. *Meetis*, Proem. Meats. It means also *properly*, MS. Ed. II. 21. Chaucer.

Myng. 68. MS. Ed. 30. *ming*, 76. *meng*, 127. 158. MS. Ed. 32. Chaucer. to mix. So *mung*, 192. is to stir. Wiclif. v. Mengyng. A. S. menʒan.

Morow. at Morow. 72. in the Morning. MS. Ed. 33. a Morrow, Chaucer. on the Morow. Lel. Coll. IV. p. 234.

Makke. 74. a dish.

Meel, Mele. 86. 97. Meal. *Melis*, Meals. Chaucer. Belg. *Meel.*

Macrows. 62. Maccharone. vide ad locum.

Makerel. 106.

2   Muskles,

Muſkles, Muſkels. 122. Muſcles. A. S. muſcule.

Malard, Maulard. 141. meaning, I preſume, both ſexes, as ducks are not otherwiſe noticed. Holme, III. p. 77. and Mr. Topham's MS.

Mylates, whyte. 153. a diſh of pork, 155.

Myddell. 170. midle. *myddes.* 175. the ſame.

Mawe. 176. Stomach of a Swine. Chaucer. Junii Etym.

Moold 177. Mould.

Maziozame. 191. Marjoram. See the various ortho-graphies in Junius, v. Majoram.

Male Marrow. 195. qu.

Moyle. v. Ris. v. Fronchemoyle.

Mulberries. 99. 132. v. Morree.

Myce, myſe. MS. Ed. 8. 15. mince myed. II. 19. minced. ymyed, 35. for ymyced. myney, II. 3. myneyd, II. 1.

Mo. MS. Ed. 38. more. Chaucer.

Maner. *of* omitted. MS. Ed. 45. 47, 48. II. 2. 28.

Mad, ymad. MS. Ed. II. 9. made.

Mychil. MS. Ed. 48. much. Chaucer. v. moche. Junius v. mickel.

Myntys. MS. Ed. II. 15. Mint. *Myntys,* Brit.

N.

A Noſt. 1. craſis of *an Oſte,* or Kiln; frequent in Kent, where *Hop-oſte* is the kiln for drying hops. ' Ooſt or Eaſt: the ſame that kiln or kill, Somer- ' ſetſhire, and elſewhere in the weſt,' Ray. So *Brykhoſt* is a Brick-kiln in Old Pariſh-Book of *Wye* in Kent, 34 H. VIII. ' We call *eſt* or *oſt* the place in ' the houſe, where the ſmoke ariſeth; and in ſome ' manors *auſtrum* or *oſtrum* is that, where a fixed ' chimney or flew anciently hath been,' Ley, in Hearne's Cur. Diſc. p. 27. *Mannors* here means, I ſuppoſe,

ſuppoſe manor-houſes, as is common in the north.
Hence *Haiſter*, for which ſee Northumb. Book,
p. 415. 417. and Chaucer. v. Eſtris.

Noumbles. 11. 13. Entrails of any beaſt, but confined now to thoſe of a deer. I ſufpeᴄt a craſis in
the caſe, quaſi *an Umble*, ſingular for what is plural
now, from Lat. *Umbilicus*. We at this day both
ſay and write *Umbles*. *Nombles*, MS. Ed. 12.
where it is *Nomblys of the venyſon*, as if there were
other Nomblys beſide. The Fr. write Nombles.

Non. 68. no. Chaucer. A. S. nan.

Nyme. 114. take, *recipe*. Sax. niman. Chaucer. uſed
in MS. Ed. throughout. See Junius. v. Nim.

Notys. 144. Wallenotes, 157. So *Not*, MS. Ed. II.
30. Chaucer. Belg. *Note*.

Nyſebek. 173. a diſh. quaſi, nice for the *Bec*, or
Mouth.

Nazt, nozt. MS. Ed. 37. not.

O.

Oynons. 2. 4. 7. Fr. Oignons. Onions.

Orage. 6. Orache.

Other, oother. 13, 14. 54. 63. MS Ed. ſæpe. Chaucer.
Wiclif. A. S. opeɲ. or.

On, oon. 14. 20. alibi. in. as in the Saxon. *One* MS.
Ed. 58. II. 21. Chaucer.

Obleys. 24. a kind of Wafer. v. ad loc.

Onys. MS. Ed. 37. once. *ones*, Chaucer. v. *Atones*,
and *ones*.

Onoward, onaward. 24. 29. 107. onward, upon it.

Of. omitted, as powder Gynger, powder Gylofre,
powder Galyngale. abounds, v. Lytel.

Oot. 26. alibi. Oat. Otyn. MS. Ed. II. Oaten.

Opyn. MS. Ed. 28. open.

Offall. 143. *Exta*, Giblets.

T

Oyſtryn.

Oyſtryn. MS. Ed. II. 14. Oyſters.
Of. Proem. by.
Ochepot. v. Hochepot.
Ovene. 1. Oven. A. S. oꝼen. Belg. Oven. *Ovyn*, MS. Ed. II. 16.
Olyve, de Olyve, Olyf, Dolyf, MS. Ed. Olive.
Owyn. MS. Ed. 22. own.

P.

Plurals increaſe a ſyllable, Almandys, Yolkys, Cranys, Pecokys, &c. So now in Kent in words ending in *ſt*. This is Saxon, and ſo Chaucer.
Plurals in *n*, Piſyn, Hennyn, Appelyn, Oyſtrin.
Powdō douce. 4. Pref.
Powdō fort. 10, 11. v. Pref.
Paſturnakes. 5. ſeems to mean *Parſnips* or Carrots, from *Paſtinaca*. *Paſternak of Raſens*. 100. of Apples, 149. means Paſtes, or Paties.
Perſel. 6. 29. alibi. *Perſele* MS. Ed. II. 15. Fr. *Perſil*. Parſley. Parcyle. MS. Ed. 32.
Pyke, pike. 18. 76. pick. Chaucer. v. Pik.
Pluk. 76. pluck, pull. A. S. pluccian.
Pellydore. 19. v. ad loc.
Peletour. 104. v. ad 19.
Paaſt. MS. Ed. II. 29. Paſte.
Potell. 20. Pottle.
Pynes. 20. alibi. v. Pref.
Pecys. 21. alibi. *Pece*, 190. *Pecis*, MS. Ed. 12. Chaucer. Pieces, Piece. 1.
Pep 21. 132. MS. Ed. 16. has *Pepyr*. Pip. 140 143. MS. Ed. 9. *Pepper*. A. S. peopoꞃ and pipoꞃ.
Papdele 24. a kind of ſauce. probably from *Papp*, a kind of *Panada*.
Piſe, Piſyn. MS. Ed. 2. Peaſe.

Peers.

Peers. 130. 138. *Pers,* 167. Perys, MS. Ed. II. 23. Pears. Pery, a Pear tree, Chaucer.

Poffynet. 30. 160. a Pofnet.

Partruches. 35. 147 *Partyches,* Contents. Partridges. *Perteryche.* E. of Devon s Feaft.

Panne. 39. 50. a Pan. A. S. Panna.

Payndemayn. 60. 139. where it is *pared.* Flour. 41. 162. 49. white Bread. Chaucer. Par. MS. Ed. 19. pare.

Peions. 18. 154. Pigeons. If you take *i* for *j*, it an-fwers to modern pronunciation, and in E. of Devon's Feaft it is written *Pejonns,* and *Pyjonns.*

Pynnonade. 51. from the Pynes of which it is made. v. Pynes. *Pynade* or *Pivade.* MS. Ed. II. 32.

Pryk. 53. prick.

Peftels. 56. Legs. We now fay *the Peftels of a lark.* of ven'fon, Lel. Colleft. IV. p. 5. Qu. a corruption of *Pedeftals.*

Payn foindew. 59. *fondew,* Contents. v. ad loc.

Pefkodde. 65. Hull or Pod of Peafe, ufed ftill in the North. v. Coddis in Wiclif, and Coddes in Junii Etymolog.

Payn Ragon. 67. a difh. qu.

Payn puff, or puf. 196. *Payne puffe.* E. of Devon's Feaft.

Pownas. 68. a colour. qu. v. Preface.

Porpays, Porpeys. 69. 108. falted, 116. roafted, 78. *Porpus* or Porpoife. *Porpecia,* Spelm. Gl. v. Geaf-pecia, which he correfts *Seafpecia.* It is furprifing he did not fee it muft be *Grafpecia* or *Crafpifcis,* i. e. *Gros* or *Craffus Pifcis,* any large fifh; a common term in charters, which allow to religious houfes or others the produce of the fea on their coafts. See Du Cange in vocibus. We do not ufe the Porpoife now, but both thefe and Seals occur in Archb. Nevill's Feaft. See Rabelais, IV. c. 60. and I conceive that the *Balæna* in Mr. Topham's MS. means the Porpus.

Perrey. 70. v. ad loc.

Pefon.

Pefõn. 70, 71. *Pife, Pifyn.* MS. Ed. 2. Peafe. Brit. *Pyfen.*

Partye. 71. *a partye,* i. e. fome. MS. Ed. 2. Chaucer.

Porrectes. 76. an herb. v. ad loc.

Purflarye. 76. Purflain.

Pochee. 90. a difh of poached Eggs. v. Junius, voce *Poach.*

Powche. 94. Crop or Stomach of a fifh. *Paunches,* 114, 115.

Pyke. 101. the fifh. v. ad loc.

Plays. 101. 103. 112. Plaife; the fifh. *Places,* Lel. Coll. VI. p. 6.

Pelettes. 112. Balls, Pellets. Pelotys. MS. Ed. 16.

Paunch. v. Powche.

Penne. 116. a Feather, or Pin. MS. Ed. 28. Wiclif. v. Pennes.

Pekok. 147. Peacock. *Pekokys,* MS. Ed. 4. where fame direction occurs. Pekok. Lel. Coll. IV. p, 227.

pffe. 150. to prefs. Chaucer.

Pyner. 155. qu. v. Pref.

Prunes. 164. Junius in v. *Prunes and Damyfyns.* 167. *Prunes Damyfyns.* 156. 158. *Primes,* 169. fhould be corrected *Prunes.* Prunys, MS. Ed. II. 17 *Prognes.* Lel. Coll. VI. p. 17. *Prune Orendge,* an Orange Plumb, p. 23. *Prones,* Northumb. Book, p. 19. plant it with Prunes, 167. ftick it, Lel. Coll. VI. p. 5. 16. 22. As the trade with Damafcus is mentioned in the Preface, we need not wonder at finding the Plumbs here.

Primes. v. Prunes.

Prews of gode paft. 176. qu

Potews. 177. a difh named from the pots ufed.

Pety puant. 195. *Petypanel, a marchpayne.* Lel. Coll. VI. p. 6.

Parade. hole parade. 195. qu.

Plater. MS. Ed. II. 9. Platter.

Puff. v. Payn.

Phifik. Proem. Phyfick.

Pome-

Pomegarnet. 84. Poungarnetts, MS. Ed. 39. Powmis
gernatys. Ibid. 27. Pomgranates, per metathefin.
Penche. MS. Ed. 36.
Partyns. MS. Ed. 38. Parts.
Pommedorry. MS. Ed. 42. Poundorroge, 58. *Pomes
endoryd.* E. of Devon's Feaft.
Pommys morles. MS. Ed. II. 3.
Porreyne. MS. Ed. II. 17. Porrey Chapeleyn, 29.

Q.

Quare. 5. It feems to mean to quarter, or to fquare,
to cut to pieces however, and may be the fame as
to *dyce.* 10. 60   Dice at this time were very
fmall : a large parcel of them were found under the
floor of the hall of one of the Temples, about
1764, and were fo minute as to have dropt at times
through the chinks or joints of the boards.   There
were near 100 pair of ivory, fcarce more than two
thirds as large as our modern ones.   The hall was
built in the reign of Elizabeth.   To *quare* is from
the Fr. quarrer; and *quayre* or *quaire,* fubft. in
Chaucer, Skelton, p. 91. 103. is a book or pam-
phlet, from the paper being in the quarto form.
See Annal. Dunftap. p. 215. Ames, Typ. Antiq.
p. 3. 9. Hence our quire of paper.   The later
French wrote *cahier, cayer,* for I prefume this may
be the fame word.   Hence, *kerve hem to dyce,* into
fmall fquares, 12. *Dyfis,* MS. Ed. 15.
Quybibes. 64. Quibibz. MS. Ed. 54. alibi. Cubebs.
Quentlich. 162. keyntlich, 189. nicely, curioufly.
Chaucer. v. *Queintlie.*
Quayle. 162. perhaps, cool. it feems to mean fail or
mifcarry. Lel. Coll. VI. p. 11. fink or be dejeſted,
p. 41. See Junius, v. Quail.
Queynchehe. 173. f. queynch. but qu.

R.

R.

R. and its vowel are often tranfpofed. v. Bryddes, brēnyng, Crudds, Pomegarnet, &c.

Rapes. 5. Turneps. Lat. *Rapa*, or *Rapum*. vide Junium in voce.

Ryfe. 9. 194. Rys, 36. alibi. MS. Ed. 14. Ryys, 192. the Flower, 37. Rice. Fr. Ris. Belg. Riis.

Roo. 14. Roe, the animal.

Rede. 21. alibi. red. A. S. ꞃeaꝺ.

Rooſt. 30. alibi. rowſted, 175. fubſtantive, 53. to roſt. Belg. rooſten.

Rether. MS. Ed. 43. a beaſt of the horned kind.

Ramme. 33. to fqueeze. but qu.

Renyns. 65. perhaps, *rennyng*, i. e. thin, from *renne*, to run. Leland Itin. I. p. 5, 6. alibi. Skelton, p. 96. 143. alibi. indeed moſt of our old authors. Lel. Coll. IV. p. 287, 288. Chaucer.

Ruayn. v. Chefe.

Rape. 83. a difh with no turneps in it. Quære if fame as *Rapil*, Holme III. p. 78. Rapy, MS. Ed. 49.

Refmolle. 96. a difh. v. ad loc.

Ryal. 99. *ryalleſt*. Proem. royal. Lel. Coll. IV. p. 250. 254. VI. p. 5. bis. 22. Chaucer. v. Rial.

Rote. 100. Root. *Rotys*, MS. Ed. 32. Chaucer. Junius, v. Root.

Roo Broth. MS. Ed. 53.

Roche. 103. the fifh. Lel. Coll. VI. p. 6.

Rygh. 105. a fifh. perhaps the Ruffe.

Rawnes. 125. Roes of fifh. *Lye* in Junius. v. Roan.

Reſt. MS. Ed. ruſtied, of meat. Reſtyn, reſtyng. Nº 57 Ruſtinefs. Junius. v. Reſtie.

Rafyols 152. a difh. *Ranfoles*. Holme III. p. 84.

Reyn. MS. Ed. 57. Rain. Chaucer.

Ryſhews. 182. name of a difh. qu.

Rew de Rumfey. MS. Ed. 44.

Ryne hem on a Spyt. 187. run them on a ſpit.

Roſty. MS. Ed. 44. roſt.

Roñde. 196. round. French.

Roſee. 52. a diſh. v. ad loc.

Reſeñs. 100. Rayſons, 114. Raiſins. uſed of Currants, 14. v. ad loc. *Reyſons, Reyſins.* MS. Ed. II. 23. 42. *Raſſens* Pottage, is in the ſecond courſe at archp. Nevill's Feaſt.

S.

Spine. v. Spynee.

Sue forth. 3. et paſſim. ſūe. 6. 21. From this ſhort way of writing, and perhaps ſpeaking, we have our *Sewers,* officers of note. and *ſewingeis,* ſerving, Lel. Coll. IV. p. 291. unleſs miſ-written or miſ-printed for *ſhewinge.*

Slype. 11. ſlip or take off the outer coat. A. S. ſlipan.

Skyrwates. 5. 149. Skirrits or Skirwicks.

Savory. 6. Sauay. 30. 63. Sawey. 172.

Self. 13. ſame, made of itſelf, as ſelf-broth, 22. the owne broth, 122. MS. Ed. 5. 7. Chaucer.

Seth. paſſim. MS. Ed. 1, 2. Chaucer to ſeeth. A. S. ſeoðan. Seyt. MS. Ed. 1. to ſtrain. 25. 27.

Smite and ſmyte. 16. 21. 62. cut, hack. A. S. ſmitan.

Sode. v. Yſode.

Storchon. MS. Ed. II. 12. v. Fitz-Stephen. p. 34.

Sum. 20. ſumdell, 51. ſomdel, 171. ſome, a little, ſome part. Chaucer has *ſum;* and *ſomdele.* A. S. ſum.

Sañders. 20. uſed for colouring. MS. Ed. 34. v. Northumb. Book, p. 415. Sandall wood. The tranſlators of that very modern book the Arabian Nights Entertainments, frequently have *Sanders* and Sandal wood, as a commodity of the Eaſt.

Swyne. 146. alibi. Pork or Bacon. MS. Ed. 3. Bacon, on the contrary, is ſometimes uſed for the animal. Old Plays, II. p. 248. Gloſſ. ad X Script. in v.

See. MS. Ed. 56. Sea. Chaucer.

Sawge, 29. *Sauge,* 160. MS. Ed. 53. Sage. *Pigge en Sage.* E. of Devon's Feaſt.   Shul.

Shul. 146. fchul. MS. Ed. 4. fhould, as N° 147.
fchulle, fchullyn. MS. Ed. 3. 7.

Sawfe Madame. 30. qu. Sauce.

Sandale. MS. Ed. 34.

Sawfe Sarzyne. 84. v. ad loc.

Serpell. 140. wild Thyme. *Serpyllum.*

Sawfé blancke. 136.

Sawfe noyre: 137. 141.

Sawfe verde. 140.

Sow. 30. to few; *fuere.* alfo 175. A. S. ſıpıan.

Stoppe. 34. 48. to ftuff.

Swyng. 39. 43. alibi. MS. Ed. 20. 25. alibi. to fhake;
mix. A. S. ſpenȝan.

Sewe. 20. 29. 40. Sowe. 30. 33. alibi. MS. Ed. 38
Chaucer. Liquor, Broth, Sous. Wiclif. A. S. ſeaꝑ.
v. Lye in 2d alphabet.

Schyms. MS. Ed. 38. Pieces.

Stondyng. 45, 46. 7. ftiff, thick.

Smale. 53. alibi. fmall. Lel. Coll. IV. p. 194.

Spynee. 57. v. ad loc.

Straw. 58. ftrew. A. S. ſꞇpeaꝑıan.

Sklyfe. 59. a Slice, or flat Stick for beating any thing.
Junius. v. Sclife.

Siryppe. 64. v. ad loc.

Styne. 66. perhaps to clofe. v. yftyned. A. S. ꞇynan.

Stere. 67. 145. to ftir. Chaucer. A. S. ſꞇýꝑıan.

Sithen. 68. ffithen, 192. then. Chaucer. v. feth and
fithe. A. S. ſıðða n. fithtyn, fethe, feth, fyth. MS.
Ed. *then.*

Salat. 76 a Sallad. Saladis, Sallads. Chaucer. Junius;
v. *Salad.*

Slete Soppes. 80. flit. A. S. ſlıꞇan.

Sprying. 85. to fprinkle. Wiclif. v fprenge. A. S.
ſpnenȝan.

Samon. 98. Salmon. So Lel. Coll. VI. p. 16, 17. Fr.
Saumon.

Stepid. 109, 116. fteeped. *Frifiis,* flippen.

Sex

Sex. 113. 176. Six. A. S.

Sool. 119. *Solys,* 133. Soale, the fish.

Schyl oysters. 121 to shell them. A. S. ʃcӱll, a shell.

Sle. 126. to kill. *Scle,* Chaucer. and *slea.* A. S. ʃlean.

Sobre Sawse. 130.

Sowpes. 82. 129. Sops. A S. ʃop. dorry. MS. Ed. II. 6.

Spell. 140. qu.

Stary. MS. Ed. 32. stir.

Swannes. 143. Pye, 79. Cygnets. Lel. Coll. VI. p. 5.

Sonne. MS. Ed. 56. Sun. Chaucer.

Sarse, and *a Sarse.* 145. a Sieve or Searse.

Souple. 152. supple. *sople,* Chaucer; also *souple.* Fr.

Stewes. 157. 170. Liquor. to stue, 186. a term well
known at this day.

Sars. 158. 164. Error perhaps for *Fars.* 167. 169.
172.

Sawcyster. 160. perhaps, a Saussage. from Fr. *Saucisse.*

Soler. MS. Ed. 56. a solar or upper floor. Chaucer.

Sawgeat. 161. v. ad loc.

Skymō. 162. a Skimmer.

Salwar. 167. v. Calwar.

Sarcynɛss. MS. Ed. 54. v. Sawse.

Syve, Seve. MS. Ed. II. 17, 18. a Sieve. v. Hersyve.

Southrenwode. 172. Southernwood.

Sowre. 173. sour. *souir,* Chaucer.

Stale. 177. Stalk. Handle. used now in the North, and
elsewhere; as a fork-stale; quære a crasis for a fork's
tail. Hence, Shaft of an Arrow. Lel. Coll. VI.
p. 13. Chaucer. A. S. ʃⱦele, or ʃⱦela.

Spot. MS. Ed. 57. Sprinkle.

Sachus. 178. a dish. v. ad loc.

Sachellis. 178. Bags. Satchells.

Spynoches. 180 Spinages. Fr. Espinars in plural. but
we use it in the singular. Ital. Spinacchia.

Sit. 192. adhere, and thereby to burn to it. It ob-
tains this sense now in the North, where, after the
potage has acquired a most disagreeable taste by it,

U

it

it is faid to be *pot-fitten*, which in Kent and elfewhere is expreffed by being *burnt-to*.

Sotiltees. Proem. Suttlety. Lel. Coll. VI. p. 5. feq.
See N° 189. There was no grand entertainment
without thefe. Lel Coll. IV. p. 226, 227. VI. 21.
feq. made of fugar and wax. p. 31. and when they
were ferved, or brought in, *at firft*, they feem to
have been called *warners*, Lel. Coll. VI. p. 21. 23.
VI. p. 226, 227. as giving *warning* of the approach
of dinner See Notes on Northumb. Book, p. 422,
423. and Mr. Pennant's Brit. Zool. p 496. There
are three *fotiltes* at the E. of Devon's Feaſt, a ſtag, a
man, a tree. Quere if now fucceeded by figures
of birds &c. made in lard, and jelly, or in fugar,
to decorate cakes.

Sewyng. Proem. following. Leland Coll. IV. p. 293.
Chaucer. Fr. *Suivre*.

Spete. MS. Ed. 28. Spit. made of hazel, 58. as
Virg. Georg. II. 396.

States. Proem. Perfons.

Scher. MS. Ed. 25. fheer, cut. Chaucer. v. Shere.

Schyveris. MS. Ed. 25. II. 27. Shivers. Chaucer. v
Slivere.

Schaw. MS. Ed. 43. fhave.

T.

Thurgh. 3. alibi. thorough. A. S. ðurh. *thorw*. MS.
Ed. II.

Tanfey. 172. Herb. vide Junii Etymol.

Trape, Trāp. 152. alibi. Pan, platter, difh. from Fr.

To gedre. 14. to gydre, 20. to gyder, 39. to gyd,
53. to gider, 59. to gyd, 111. to gedr, 145. So
varioufly is the word *together* here written. A. S.
toȝaðene.

Tredure. 15. name of Cawdel. v. ad loc.

To. 30. 17. MS. Ed. 33. 42. too; and fo the Saxon.
Hence to to. 17. v. ad loc. Alfo, Lel. Coll. IV.

I

p. 181. 206. VI. p. 36. *To* is *till*, MS. Ed. 26. 34. *two*. II. 7. v. Unʃo.

Thyk. 20. a Verb, to grow thick, as Nº 67. thicken taken paʃʃively. Adjective, 29. 52. *thik*, 57. *thykke*, 85. *thike*, Chaucer.

Teyʃe. 20. to pull to pieces with the fingers. v. ad loc. et Junius, voce Teaʃe. Hence teaʃing for carding wool with teaʃels, a ʃpecies of thiʃtle or inʃtrument.

Talbotes. 23. qu. v. ad loc.

Tat. 30. that. as in Derbyʃh. *who's tat ?* for, who is that ? Belg. *dat*.

Thenne. 36 alibi. then. Chaucer. A. S. ꝺanne.

Thanne. 36. MS. Ed. 25. then. A. S. ꝺan. than. MS. Ed. 14.

Teer. 36. Tear. A. S. ꞇeꞃan.

To fore. 46. alibi. before. Hence our *heretofore*. Wiclif. Chaucer. A. S. ꞇoꝼoꞃan.

Thynne. 49. MS. Ed. 15. thin. A. S. ꝺinn.

Tarlettes. 50. afterwards *Tartletes*, rectiùs; and ʃo the Contents. *Tortelletti*. Holme p. 85. v. Tartee. Godwin, de Præʃul. p. 695. renders *Streblitæ* ; et v. Junius, voce Tart.

Thiʃe. 53. alibi. theʃe.

Take. 56. taken. Chaucer.

Thridde. 58. 173. alibi. Third, per metatheʃin. Chaucer. Thriddendele, 67. Thriddel, 102. 134. *Thredde*, MS. Ed. II. 1. v. Junius, voce Thirdendeal.

To done. 68. done. *To* ʃeems to abound, vide Chaucer. v. *To*.

Turneʃole. 68. colours *pownas*. vide ad loc.

Ther. 70. 74. they. Chaucer.

Ton treʃʃis. 76. an herb. I amend it to *Ton creʃʃis*, and explain it *Creʃʃes*, being the Saxon ꞇunkepꞃe, or ꞇuncæpꞃe. See *Lye*, Dict. Sax. Creʃʃes, ʃo as to mean, *one of the Creʃʃes*.

Turbut. 101.

Tried out. 117. drawn out by roaʃting. See Junius, v. Try.

Tweydel.

Tweydel. 134. Twey, MS. Ed. 12. Chaucer. *Twy*
for *Twice* runs now in the North. A. S. ʧpa, two.
Oæl, pars, portio.

Talow. 159 Mutton Sewet. v. Junii Etym.

Thyes, Thyes MS. Ed. 29, 30. Thighs.

Tartee. 164, 165. alibi. Tart. de Bry, 166. de Brymlent, 187. Tartes of Flefh, 168. of Fifh, 170. v.
Tarlettes.

Towh. tough, thick. 173. See Chaucer. v. Tought.
A. S. ʧoh.

Tharmys. MS. Ed. 16. Rops, Guts.

There. 170. 177 where. Chaucer.

Thowche. MS. Ed. 48. touch.

To. 185. for. Hence, *wherto* is *wherefore*. Chaucer.

Towayl. MS. Ed. II 21. a Towel.

Thee. 189. thou, as often now in the North.

Temper. MS. Ed. 1. et fæpe. to mix.

U.

Uppon. 85. alibi. upon.

Urchon, 176. Urchin, *Erinaceus.*

Unto. MS. Ed. 2. until. v. *To.* Chaucer.

V.

Violet. 6. v. ad loc.

Verjous. 12. 48. viaws. 154. verious. 15. Verjuice,
Fr. Verjus. V. Junium.

Veel. 16. alibi. MS. Ed. 18. Veal.

Vefsll. 29. a difh.

Vyne Grace. 61. a mefs or difh. *Grees* is the wild
Swine. Plott, Hift. of Staff. p. 443. Gloff. to Doug-
las' Virgil. v. Grifis. and to Chaucer. v. Grys.
Thoroton, p. 258. Blount, Tenures. p. 101. *Greffe.*
                                                    Lel.

Lel. Coll. IV. p. 243. *Gres.* 248. Both pork and wine enter into the recipe.

Vyānde Cypre. 97. from the Ifle of Cyprus.

Vernage. 132. Vernaccia. a fort of Italian white-wine. In Pref. to *Perlin,* p. xix. mif-written Vervage. See Chaucer. It is a fweet wine in a MS. of Tho. Aftle efq. p. 2.

Venyfon. 135. often eaten with furmenty, E. of Devon's Feaft. *in brothe.* Ibid.

Verde Sawfe. 140. it founds *Green Sauce,* but there is no forel ; fharp, four Sauce. See Junius, v. Verjuice.

Vervayn. 172.

W.

Wele. 1. 28. old pronunciation of *well,* now vulgarly ufed in Derbyfh. *wel,* 3. alibi. *wel fmale,* 6. very fmall. v. Lel. Coll. IV. p. 218. 220. Hearne, in Spelm. Life of Ælfred. p. 96.

Wyndewe. 1. winnow. This pronunciation is ftill retained in Derbyfhire, and is not amifs, as the operation is performed by wind. v. omnino, Junius. v. Winnow.

Wayfhe, waifsh, waifche. 1. 5. 17. to wafh. A. S. pæɼcan.

Whane, whan. 6. 23. 41. when. So Sir Tho. Elliot. v. Britannia. Percy's Songs, I. 77. MS. Romance of Sir Degare verf. 134. A. S. hɼænne. wan, wanne. MS. Ed. 25. 38. when.

Wole. Proem. will. *wolt.* 68. wouldft. Chaucer. v. Wol.

Warly, Warliche. 20. 188. gently, warily. A. S. pæɲe, wary, prudent. Chaucer. v. Ware. Junius, v. Warie.

Wafroñs. 24. Wafers. Junius, v. Wafer.

With

With inne. 30. divifim, for within. So *with oute*, 33.

Welled. 52. v. ad loc. MS. Ed. 23.

Wete. 67. 161. wet, now in the North, and fee Chaucer. A. S. ꝑæꞇ.

Wry. 72. to dry, or cover. Junius, v. Wrie.

Wyn. MS. Ed. 22. alibi. Wine. v. Wyneger.

Wryng thurgh a Straynour. 81. 91. thurgh a cloth, 153. almandes with fair water, 124. wryng out the water. Ibid. wryng parfley up with eggs, 174. Chaucer, voce wrong, ywrong, and wrang. Junius, v. Wring.

Womdes, Wombes. 107. quære the former word? perhaps being falfely written, it was intended to be obliterated, but forgotten. *Wombes* however means *bellies*, as MS. Ed. 15. See Junius, voce *Womb*.

Wyneger. MS. Ed. 50. Vinegar. v. Wyn.

Wone. 107. *a deal* or *quantity*. Chaucer. It has a contrary fenfe though in Junius, v. Whene.

Whete. 116. Wete. MS. Ed. 1. II. 30. Wheat. A. S. hꝑæꞇe.

Waftel. 118. white Bread. *yfarced*, 159. of it. MS. Ed. 30. II. 18. Gloff. ad X Script. v. Simenellus. Chaucer; where we are referred to Verftegan V. but *Waffel* is explained there, and not *Waftel*; however, fee Stat. 51 Henry III. Hoveden, p. 738. and Junius' Etymol.

Wheyze. 150. 171. Whey. A. S. hꝑæz. Serum Lactis. g often diffolving into y. v. Junium, in Y.

Wynde it to balles. 152. make it into balls, turn it. Chaucer. v. Wende. Junius, v. Winde.

Wallenotes. 157. Walnuts. See Junius, in voce.

Wofe of Comtrey. 190. v. ad loc. Juice.

Wex. MS. Ed. 25. Wax.

Were. MS. Ed. 57. where.

Y.

Y.

Y. is an ufual prefix to adjectives and participles in
our old authors. It came from the Saxons; hence
ymynced,'minced; yflyt, flit; &c. *I* is often fub-
ftituted for it. V. Gloff. to Chaucer, and Lye in
Jun. Etym. v. I.

    It occurs perpetually for *i*, as ymynced, yflyt, &c.
and fo in MS. Editoris alfo.

    Written z. 7. 18. alibi. ufed for *gh*, 72. MS. Ed.
33. Chaucer. v. Z. Hence ynouhz, 22. enough.
So MS. Ed. paffim. Quere if *z* is not meant
in MSS for g or *t* final.

    Dotted, y, after Saxon manner, in MS. Ed. as in
Mr. Hearne's edition of Robt. of Gloucefter.

Ycorve. 100, 101. cut in. pieces. icorvin, 133. Gloff.
to Chaucer. v. *Icorvin*, and *Throtycorve*.

Zelow. 194. *yolow*. MS. Ed. 30. yellow. A.S. zealure
and zelep.

Yolkes. 18. i. e. of eggs. Junius, v. Yelk.

Ygrond. v. Gronden.

Yleefshed. 18. cut it into flices. So, *lefh* it, 65. 67.
leach is to flice, Holme III. p. 78. or it may mean
to *lay in the difh*, 74. 81. or diftribute, 85. 117.

Ynouhz. 22. ynowh, 23. 28. ynowh, 65. ynow.
MS. Ed. 32. Enough. Chaucer has *inough*.

Yfer. 22. 61. id eft *ifere*, together. *Feer*, a Companion.
Wiclif, in *Feer* and *Scukynge-feer*. Chaucer. v. Fere,
and Yfere. Junius, v. Yfere.

Yfette. Proem. put down, written.

Yfkaldid. 29. fcalded.

Yfode. 29. *ifode*, 90. *fodden*, 179. boiled. MS. Ed. II.
11. Chaucer. all trom to feeth.

Yfope. 30. 63. Yfop. MS. Ed. 53. the herb Hyffop.
Chaucer. v. Ifope.

Yforced. v. forced.

Yfafted. 62. qu.

Zif,

Zif, zyf. MS. Ed. 37. 39. if. alſo give, II. 9. 10.

Yſtyned, iſtyned. 162. 168. to *ſyne*, 66. ſeems to mean to cloſe.

Yteyſed. 20. pulled in pieces. v. ad loc. and v. Teaſe.

Ypānced. 62. perhaps pounced, for which ſee Chaucer.

Yfondred. 62. *ifonded*, 97. 102. *yfondyt*, 102. poured, mixed, diſſolved. v. *found*. Fr. fondu.

Yholes. 37. perhaps, hollow.

Ypared. 64. pared.

Ytoſted, itoſted. 77. 82. toaſted.

Iboiled. 114. boiled.

Yeſt. 151. Junius, v. Yeaſt.

Igrated. 153. grated.

Ybake. 157. baked.

Ymbre. 160. 165. Ember.

Ypocras. how made, 191. Hippocras. wafers uſed with it. Lel. Coll. IV. p. 330. VI. p. 5, 6. 24. 28. 12. and dry toaſts, Rabelais IV. c. 59. *Joly Ypocras*. Lel. Coll. IV. p. 227. VI. p. 23. Biſhop Godwin renders it *Vinum aromaticum*. It was brought both at beginning of ſplendid entertainments, if Apicius is to be underſtood of it. Lib. I. c. 1. See Liſter, ad loc. and in the middle before the ſecond courſe; Lel. Coll. IV. p. 227. and at the end. It was in uſe at St. John's Coll. Cambr. 50 years ago, and brought in at Chriſtmas at the cloſe of dinner, as anciently moſt uſually it was. It took its name from *Hippocrates' ſleeve*, the bag or ſtrainer, through which it was paſſed. Skinner, v. Claret; and Chaucer. or as Junius ſuggeſts, becauſe ſtrained *juxta doctrinam Hippocratis*. The Italians call it *hipocraſſo*. It ſeems not to have differed much from *Piment*, or Pigment (for which ſee Chaucer) a rich ſpiced wine which was ſold by Vintners about 1250. Mr. Topham's MS. Hippocras was both white and red. Rabelais, IV. c. 59. and I find it uſed for ſauce to lampreys. Ibid. c. 60.

There

There is the procefs at large for making ypocrafle
in a MS. of my refpectable Friend Thomas Aftle, efq.
p. 2. which we have thought proper to tranfcribe, as
follows:

' To make Ypocrafle for lords with gynger,
' fynamon, and graynes fugour, and turefoll: and
' for comyn pepull gynger canell, longe peper, and
' claryffyed hony. Loke ye have feyre pewter
' bafens to kepe in your pouders and your ypocrafle
' to ren ynne. and to vi bafens ye mufte have vi
' renners on a perche as ye may here fee. and loke
' your poudurs and your gynger be redy and well
' paryd or hit be beton in to poud'. Gynger colom-
' byne is the beft gynger, mayken and balandyne
' be not fo good nor holfom. . . . now thou knowift
' the propertees of Ypocras. Your poudurs muft
' be made everyche by themfelfe, and leid in a bled-
' der in ftore, hange fure your perche with baggs,
' and that no bagge twoyche other, but bafen
' twoyche bafen. The fyrft bagge of a galon, every
' on of the other a potell. Fyrft do in to a bafen a
' galon or ij of redwyne, then put in your pouders,
' and do it in to the renners, and fo in to the feconde
' bagge, then take a pece and affay it. And yef hit
' be eny thyng to ftronge of gynger alay it withe
' fynamon, and yef it be ftrong of fynamon alay it
' withe fugour cute. And thus fchall ye make per-
' fyte Ypocras. And loke your bagges be of boltell
' clothe, and the mouthes opyn, and let it ren in
' v or vi bagges on a perche, and under every bagge
' a clene bafen. The draftes of the fpies is good for
' fewies. Put your Ypocrafe in to a ftanche weffell,
' and bynde opon the mouthe a bleddur ftrongly,
' then ferve forthe waffers and Ypocrafle.'

Y   ADDEN-

A D D E N D A.

p. i. add at bottom. ' vi. 22. where *Noah* and the
' beafts are to live on the fame food.'

xiv. after *ingeniofa gula eft*, add, ' The *Italians* now
' eat many things which we think perfect carrion.
' *Ray*, Trav. p. 362. 406. The *French* eat frogs
' and fnails. The *Tartars* feaft on horfe-flefh, the
' *Chinefe* on dogs, and meer *Savages* eat every
' thing. *Goldfmith*, Hift. of the Earth, &c. II. p. 347,
' 348. 395. III. p. 297. IV. p. 112. 121, &c.'

xviii. lin. 1. after *ninth Iliad*, add, ' And Dr. *Shaw*
' writes, p. 301, that even now in the Eaft, the
' greateft prince is not afhamed to fetch a lamb
' from his herd and kill it, whilft the princefs is
' impatient till fhe hath prepared her fire and her
' kettle to drefs it.'

Ibid. lin. 12. after *heretofore* add, ' we have fome
' good families in England of the name of *Cook* or
' *Coke*. I know not what they may think ; but we
' may depend upon it, they all originally fprang
' from real and profeffional cooks ; and they need
' not be afhamed of their extraction, any more
' than the *Butlers*, *Parkers*, *Spencers*, &c.'

xix. add at bottom, ' reflect or the Spanifh *Olio* or
' *Olla podrida*, and the French fricaffée.'

xxv. lin. ult. *intended*. add, ' See *Ray*, Trav. p. 283.
' 407. and *Wright's* Trav. p. 112.'

ADVER-

ADVERTISEMENT.

SINCE the foregoing sheets were printed off, the following very curious Rolls have happily fallen into the Editor's hand, by the favour of John Charles Brooke, Esq. Somerset Herald. They are extracted from a MS. belonging to the family of Nevile of Chevet, near Wakefield, com. Ebor. and thence copied, under the direction of the Rev. Richard Kay, D. D. Prebendary of Durham.

These Rolls are so intimately connected with our subject, as exhibiting the dishes of which our Roll of *Cury* teaches the dressing and preparation, that they must necessarily be deemed a proper appendix to it. They are moreover amusing, if not useful, in another respect; *viz.* as exhibiting the gradual prices of provisions, from the dates of our more ancient lists, and the time when these Rolls were composed, in the reign of Henry VIII. For the further illustration of this subject, an extract from the old Account-Book of *Luton*, 19 *Hen.* VIII. is super-added; where the prices of things in the South, at the same period,

may

may be feen. And whoever pleafes to go further into this matter of *prices*, may compare them with the particulars and expence of a dinner at Stationer's-Hall, A. D. 1556. which appeared in the St. James's Chronicle of April 22, 1780.

We cannot help thinking that, upon all accounts, the additions here prefented to our friends muft needs prove exceedingly acceptable to them.

ROLLS

ROLLS of PROVISIONS,

With their PRICES, DISHES, &c.

Temp. H. VIII.

THE marriage of my fon-in-law [a] Gervas Clifton and my daughter Mary Nevile, the 17th day of January, in the 21ft year of the reigne of our Soveraigne Lord King Henry the VIIIth.

	£.	s.	d.
Firft, for the apparell of the faid Gervys Clifton and Mary Nevill, 21 yards of Ruffet Damafk, every yard 8s [b],	7	14	8
Item, 6 yards of White Damafk, every yard 8s.		48	0

[a] Gervas] below *Gervys*. So unfettled was our orthography, even in the reign of Henry VIII. So *Nevile*, and below *Nevill*. Mary, third daughter of Sir John Nevil of Chevet, was firft wife of Sir Gerv. Clifton of Clifton, com. Nott. Knight.

[b] 8 s.] The fum is £. 7. 14 s. 8 d. but ought to be £. 8. 8 s. fo that there is fome miftake here. *N. B.* This tranfcript is given in our common figures; but the original, no doubt, is in the Roman.

Z   Item,

	£.	s.	d.
Item, 12 yards of Tawney Camlet, every yard 2s. 8d ^c.		49	4
Item, 6 yards of Tawney Velvet, every yard 14s.	4	4	0
Item, 2 Rolls of Buckrom,	0	6	0
Item, 3 Black Velvet Bonnits for women, every bonnit 17s.		51	0
Item, a Fronſlet ^d of Blue Velvet,	0	7	6
Item, an ounce of Damaſk Gold ^e,	0	4	0
Item, 4 Laynes ^f of Frontlets,	0	2	8
Item, an Eyye ^g of Pearl,		24	0
Item, 3 pair of Gloves,	0	2	10
Item, 3 yards of Kerſey ; 2 black, 1 white,	0	7	0
Item, Lining for the ſame,	0	2	0
Item, 3 Boxes to carry bonnits in,	0	1	0
Item, 3 Paſts ^h,	0	0	9
Item, a Furr of White Luſants ⁱ,		40	0
Item, 12 Whit Heares ^k,		12	0
Item, 20 Black Conies,		10	0

^c 2 s. 8 d.] This again is wrongly computed. There may be other miſtakes of the ſame kind, which is here noted once for all ; the reader will eaſily rectify them himſelf.

^d Fronſlet.] f. Frontlet, as lin. 10.

^e Damaſk Gold.] Gold of Damaſcus, perhaps for powder.

^f Laynes.] qu.

^g Eyye.] f. Egg.

^h Paſts.] Paſtboards.

ⁱ Luſants.] qu.

^k Heares]. f. Hares.

Item,

	£.	s.	d.
Item, A pair of Myllen [1] Sleves of white fattin,	o	8	o
Item, 30 White Lamb Skins,	o	4	o
Item, 6 yards of White Cotton,	o	3	o
Item, 2 yards and ½ black fattin,	o	14	9
Item, 2 Girdles,	o	5	4
Item, 2 ells of White Ribon, for tippets,	o	1	1
Item, an ell of Blue Sattin,	o	6	8
Item, a Wedding Ring of Gold,	o	12	4
Item, a Millen Bonnit, dreffed with Agletts,	o	11	o
Item, a yard of right White Sattin,	o	12	o
Item, a yard of White Sattin of Bridge [m],	o	2	4

The Expence of the Dinner, at the marriage of faid Gervys Clifton and Mary Nevile. Imprimis,

	£.	s.	d.
Three Hogfheads of Wine, 1 white, 1 red, 1 claret,	5	5	o
Item, 2 Oxen,	3	o	o
Item, 2 Brawns [n],	1	o	o
Item, 2 Swans [o], every Swan 2 s,	o	12	o

---

[1] Myllen]. *Milan*, city of Lombardy, whence our *millaner*, now *milliner*, written below *millen*.

[m] Bridge]. Brugge, or Bruges, in Flanders.

[n] Brawns]. The Boar is now called a Brawn in the North, vid. p. 126.

[o] 2 Swans]. f. 6 Swans.

Z 2

Item,

	£.	s.	d.
Item, 9 Cranes[p], every Crane 3 s. 4 d.	1	10	0
Item, 16 Heron fews[q], every one 12 d.	0	16	0
Item, 10 Bitterns, each 14 d.	0	11	8
Item, 60 couple of Conies, every couple 5 d,		25	0
Item, as much Wild-fowl, and the charge of the fame, as coſt	3	6	8
Item, 16 Capons of Greaſe[r],	0	16	0
Item, 30 other Capons,	0	15	0
Item, 10 Pigs, every one 5 d.	0	4	2
Item, 6 Calves,	0	16	0
Item, 1 other Calf,	0	3	0
Item, 7 Lambs,	0	10	0
Item, 6 Withers[s], every Wither 2 s. 4 d.	0	14	0
Item, 8 Quarters of Barley[t] Malt, every quarter 14 s.	5	10	0
Item, 3 Quarters of Wheat, every quarter 18 s.		54	0
Item, 4 dozen of Chickens,	0	6	0

Befides Butter, Eggs, Verjuice, and Vinegar.

---

[p] Cranes]. v. p. 67.

[q] Heron fews]. In one word, rather. See p. 139.

[r] of Greaſe.] I preſume fatted.

[s] Withers]. Weathers.

[t] Barley malt]. So diftinguifhed, becauſe wheat and oats were at this time fometimes malted. See below, p. 172.

In

In Spices as followeth.

$\mathcal{L}. \quad s. \quad d.$

Two Loaves of Sugar ᵘ; weighing 16 lb.
12 oz. at 7 d. per lb.   0   9   9

Item, 6 pound of Pepper, every pound 22d. 0   11   0

Item, 1 pound of Ginger,   0   2   4

Item, 12 pound of Currants, every pound 3½d. 0   3   6

Item, 12 lb. of Proynes ˣ, every pound 2d. 0   2   0

Item, 2 lb. of Marmalet,   0   2   1

Item, 2 ʸPoils of Sturgeon,   0   12   4

Item, a Barrel for the fame,   0   0   6

Item, 12 lb. of Dates, every lb. 4d.   0   4   0

Item. 12 lb. of Great Raisons ᶻ,   0   2   0

Item, 1 lb. of Cloves and Mace,   0   8   0

Item, 1 quarter of Saffron,   0   4   0

Item, 1 lb. of Tornfelf ᵃ,   0   4   0

Item, 1 lb. of Ising-glafs,   0   4   0

Item, 1 lb. of Bifkitts,   0   1   0

Item, 1 lb. of Carraway Seeds,   0   1   0

Item, 2 lb. of Cumfitts,   0   2   0

Item, 2 lb. of Torts ᵇ of Portugal,   0   2   0

ᵘ Loaves of Sugar]. So that they had now a method of refining
it, v. p. xxvi.

ˣ Proynes]. Prunes, v. p. 148.

ʸ Poils]. Mifread, perhaps, for Joils, *i. e.* Jowls.

ᶻ Great Raifons,] v. p. 38.

ᵃ Tornfell]. Turnfole, v. p. 38.

ᵇ Torts]. qu.

Item,

	£.	s.	d.
Item, 4 lb. of Liquorice and Annifeeds,	0	1	0
Item, 3 lb. of Green Ginger,	0	4	0
Item, 3 lb. of Suckets ᶜ,	0	4	0
Item, 3 lb. of Orange Buds, 4s.	0	5	4
Item, 4 lb. of Oranges in Syrup,	0	5	4
Totall £.	61	8	8

ᶜ Suckets]. Thefe, it feems, were fold ready prepared in the fhops. See the following Rolls.

Sir

Sir John Nevile, ⎱ The marriage of my Son-in-law,
of Chete, Knight. ⎰ Roger Rockley[a], and my daughter Elizabeth Nevile, the 14th of January, in the 17th year of the reigne of our Soveraigne Lord King Henry the VIIIth.

	£.	s.	d.
First, for the expence of their Apparel, 22 yards of Russet Sattin, at 8 s. per yard,	8	16	0
Item, 2 Mantilles of Skins, for his gown,		48	0
Item, 2 yards and ½ of black velvet, for his gown,	0	30	0
Item, 9 yards of Black Sattin, for his Jacket and Doublet, at 8 s. the yard,	3	12	0
Item, 7 yards of Black Sattin, for her Kertill, at 8 s. per yard,		56	0
Item, a Roll of Buckrom,	0	2	8
Item, a Bonnit of Black Velvet,	0	15	0
Item, a Frontlet for the same Bonnit,	0	12	0
Item, for her Smock,	0	5	0
Item, for a pair of perfumed Gloves,	0	3	4
Item, for a pair of other Gloves,	0	0	4

[a] Rockley]. Elizabeth eldest daughter of Sir John Nevile, married, Roger eldest son, and afterwards heir, of Sir Thomas Rockley of Rockley, in the parish of Worsborough, Knight.

Second

Second Day.

	£.	s.	d.
Item, for 22 yards of Tawney Camlet, at 2s. 4d. per yard,		51	4
Item, 3 yards of Black Sattin, for lining her gown, at 8s per yard,		24	0
Item, 2 yards of Black Velvet, for her gown,		30	0
Item, a Roll of Buckrom, for her Gown,	0	2	8
Item, 7 yards of Yellow Sattin Bridge[b], at 2s. 4d. per yard,		26	4
Item, for a pair of Hose,	0	2	4
Item, for a pair Shoes,	0	1	4
Sum £.	27	8	0

Item, for Dinner, and the Expence of the said Marriage of Roger Rockley, and the said Elizabeth Nevile.

	£.	s.	d.
Imprimis, eight quarters of Barley-malt, at 10s. per quarter,	4	0	0
Item, 3 quarters and ½ of Wheat, at 14s. 4d. per quarter,		56	8
Item, 2 Hogsheads of Wine, at 40s.	4	0	0
Item, 1 Hogshead of Red Wine, at	0	40	0
Sum Total £.	39	8	0

[b] Bridge]. See above, p. 167, note[m].

For

For the First Course, at Dinner.

Imprimis, Brawn with Musterd, served alone with Malmsey.

Item, Frumety ᶜ to Pottage.

Item, a Roe roasted for Standert ᵈ.

Item, Peacocks, 2 of a Dish.

Item, Swans 2 of a Dish.

Item, a great Pike in a Dish.

Item, Conies roasted 4 of a Dish.

Item, Venison roasted.

Item, Capon of Grease, 3 of a Dish.

Item, Mallards ᵉ, 4 of Dish.

Item, Teals, 7 of a Dish.

Item, Pyes baken ᶠ, with Rabbits in them.

Item, Baken Orange.

Item, a Flampett ᵍ.

Item, Stoke Fritters ʰ.

Item, Dulcets ⁱ, ten of Dish.

Item, a Tart.

ᶜ Frumety]. v. p. 135.

ᵈ Standert]. A large or standing dish. See p. 174. l. 3.

ᵉ Mallards]. v. p. 144.

ᶠ Baken]. baked.

ᵍ Flampett]. f. Flaunpett, or Flaumpeyn, v. p. 136.

ʰ Stoke Fritters]. Baked on a hot-iron, used still by the Brewers, called a stoker.

ⁱ Dulcets]. qu.

Second Courfe.

Firft, Marterns [k] to Pottage.

Item for a Standert, Cranes 2 of a difh.

Item, Young Lamb, whole roafted.

Item, Great Frefh Sammon Gollis [l].

Item, Heron Sues, 3 of a difh.

Item, Bitterns, 3 of a difh.

Item, Pheafants, 4 of a difh.

Item, a Great Sturgeon Poil.

Item, Partridges, 8 of a difh.

Item, Plover, 8 of a difh.

Item, Stints [m], 8 of a difh.

Item, Curlews [n], 3 of a difh.

Item, a whole Roe, baken.

Item, Venifon baken, red and fallow [o].

Item, a Tart.

Item, a March [p] Payne.

Item, Gingerbread.

Item, Apples and Cheefe fcraped with Sugar and Sage.

[k] Marterns]. qu. it is written Martens, below.

[l] Gollis]. f. Jowls.

[m] Stints]. The Stint, or Purre, is one of the Sandpipers. Pennant, Brit. Zool, II. 374.

[n] Curlews]. See above, p. 130. and below. Curlew Knaves, alfo below.

[o] Fallow.] If I remember right, Dr. Goldfmith fays, Fallow-deer were brought to us by King James I. but fee again below, more than once.

[p] March Payne]. A kind of Cake, very common long after this time, v. below.

For

For Night.

Firſt a Play, and ſtraight after the play a Maſk, and when the Maſk was done then the Banckett ⁹, which was 110 diſhes, and all of meat ; and then all the Gentilmen and Ladys danced; and this continued from the Sunday to the Saturday afternoon.

The Expence in the Week for Fleſh and Fiſh for the ſame marriage.

	£.	s.	d.
Imprimis, 2 Oxen,	3	0	0
Item, 2 Brawns,		22	0
Item, 2 Roes 10s. and for ſervants going, 5s.	0	15	0
Item, in Swans,	0	15	0
Item, in Cranes 9,		30	0
Item, in Peacocks 12,	0	16	0
Item, in Great Pike, for fleſh dinner, 6,		30	0
Item, in Conies, 21 dozen,	5	5	0
Item, in Veniſon, Red Deer Hinds 3, and fetching them,	0	10	0
Item, Fallow Deer Does 12,	—	—	—
Item, Capons of Greaſe 72,	3	12	0
Item, Mallards and Teal, 30 dozen,	3	11	8
Item, Lamb 3,	0	4	0
Item, Heron Sues, 2 doz.		24	0

⁹ Banckett]. Banquet.

A a 2

Item,

	£.	s.	d.
Item, Shovelords ᵣ, 2 doz.		24	0
Item, in Bytters ˢ 12,		16	0
Item, in Pheaſants 18,		24	0
Item, in Partridges 40,	0	6	8
Item, in Curlews 18,		24	0
Item, in Plover, 3 dozen,	0	5	0
Item, in Stints, 5 doz.	0	9	0
Item, in Sturgeon, 1 Goyle ᵗ,	0	5	0
Item, 1 Seal ᵘ,	0	13	4
Item, 1 Porpoſe ˣ,	0	13	4

£.

For Frydays and Saturdays.

Firſt, Leich Brayne ʸ.
Item, Frometye Pottage.

ᵣ Shovelords]. Shovelers, a ſpecies of the Wild Duck. Shove-lards, below.

ˢ Bytters]. Bitterns, above; but it is often written without *n*, as below.

ᵗ Goyle]. Jowl, v. above, p. 174. l. 5.

ᵘ Seal]. One of thoſe things not eaten now; but ſee p. 147 above, and below, p. 180. l. 6.

ˣ Porpoſe]. v. p. 147. above.

ʸ Leich Brayne]. v. p. 141, above. but qu. as to Brayne.

Item,

Item, Whole Ling and Huberdyne[z].
Item, Great Goils[a] of Salt Sammon.
Item, Great Salt Eels.
Item, Great Salt Sturgeon Goils.
Item, Freſh Ling.
Item, Freſh Turbut.
Item, Great Pike[b].
Itdm, Great Goils of Freſh Sammon.
Item, Great Ruds[c].
Item, Baken Turbuts.
Item, Tarts of 3 ſeveral meats[d].

Second Courſe.

Firſt, Martens to Pottage.
Item, a Great Freſh Sturgeon Goil.
Item, Freſh Eel roaſted.
Item, Great Brett.
Item, Sammon Chines broil'd.
Item, Roaſted Eels.
Item, Roaſted Lampreys.
Item, Roaſted Lamprons[e].
Item, Great Burbutts[f].

[z] Huberdyne]. miſwritten for Haberdine, i. e. from Aberdeen ; written below Heberdine.

[a] Goils]. v. above, p. 174. l. 5.

[b] Pyke]. v. above, p. 50. and below, often.

[c] Ruds]. qu. Roaches, v. below.

[d] meats]. Viands, but not Fleſhmeats.

[e] Lamprons]. v. p. 142, above.

[f] Burbatts]. qu. Turbuts.

Item,

Item, Sammon baken.
Item, Fresh Eel baken.
Item, Fresh Lampreys, baken.
Item, Clear Jilly [g].
Item, Gingerbread.

Waiters at the said Marriage.

Storrers, Carver.
Mr. Henry Nevile, Sewer.
Mr. Thomas Drax, Cupbearer.
Mr. George Pashlew, for the Sewer-board end.
John Merys, } Marshalls.
John Mitchill, }
Robert Smallpage, for the Cupboard.
William Page, for the Celler.
William Barker, for the Ewer.
Robert Sike the Younger, and
John Hiperon, for Butterye.

To wait in the Parlour.

Richard Thornton.
Edmund North.
Robert Sike the Elder.
William Longley.
Robert Live.
William Cook.
Sir John Burton, Steward.
My brother Stapleton's servant.
My son Rockley's servant to serve in the state.

[g] Jilly]. Jelly.

The

The Charges of Sir John Nevile, of Chete, Knight, being Sheriff of Yorkſhire in the 19th year of the reigne of King Henry VIII.

Lent Aſſizes.

	£.	s.	d.
Imprimis, in Wheat 8 quarters,	8	0	0
Item, in Malt, 11 quarters,	7	6	8
Item, in Beans, 4 quarters,	3	4	0
Item, in Hay, 6 loads,		25	0
Item, in Litter, 2 loads,	0	4	0
Item, part of the Judge's Horſes in the inn,	0	13	4
Item, 5 hogſheads of Wine, 3 claret, 1 white, 1 red,	10	16	4
Item, Salt Fiſh, 76 couple,	3	16	4
Item, 2 barrells Herrings,		25	6
Item, 2 Barrells Salmon,	3	1	0
Item, 12 ſeams ª of Sea Fiſh,	6	4	0
Item, in Great Pike and Pickering, 6 ſcore and 8,	8	0	0
Item, 12 Great Pike from Ramſay,	2	0	0
Item, in Pickerings from Holdeſs IIII xx,	3	0	0
Item, Received of Ryther 20 great Breams,		20	0
Item, Received of ſaid Ryther, 12 great Tenches,	0	16	0

ª ſeams]. quarter, much uſed in Kent, v. infra.

Item,

	£.	s.	d.
Item, Received of said Ryther 12 great Eels and 106 Touling [b] Eels, and 200 lb. of Brewit [c] Eels, and 20 great Ruds,		40	0
Item, in great Fresh Sammon, 28	3	16	8
Item, a Barrell of Sturgeon,		46	8
Item, a Firkin of Seal,	0	16	8
Item, a little barrell of Syrope [d],	0	6	8
Item, 2 barrells of all manner of Spices,	4	10	0
Item, 1 bag of Isinglass,	0	3	0
Item, a little barrell of Oranges,	0	4	0
Item, 24 gallons of Malmsey,	0	16	0
Item, 2 little barrells of Green Ginger and Sucketts,	0	3	0
Item, 3 Bretts,	0	12	0
Item, in Vinegar, 13 gallon, 1 quart	0	6	8
Item, 8 large Table Cloths of 8 yards in length, 7 of them 12 d per yard, and one 16 d,	3	6	8
Item, 6 doz. Manchetts [e],	0	6	0
Item, 6 gallons Vergis [f],	0	4	8
Item, in Mayne Bread [g],	0	0	8

[b] Touling Eels]. qu. see below.

[c] Brewit Eels]. *i. e.* for Brewet ; for which see above, p. 127. also here, below.

[d] Syrope]. v. p. 36. above.

[e] Manchetts]. a species of Bread, see below.

[f] Vergis]. Verjuice.

[g] Mayne Bread]. Pain du main, v. p. 147. above.

Item

	£.	s.	d.
Item, bread bought for March Payne,	o	o	8
Item, for Sugar and Almonds, befides the 2 barrels,	o	11	o
Item, for Salt	o	6	o
Item, for 5 gallons of Muftard,	o	2	6
Item, a Draught of Fifh, 2 great Pikes and 200 Breams,	o	26	8
Item, 3 gallons of Honey,	o	3	9
Item, 6 Horfe-loads of Charcoal,	o	2	8
Item, 3 Load of Talwood h and Bavings,	o	3	4
Item, 4 Streyners,	o	1	o
Item, for Graines i,	o	o	4
Item, 20 doz. of Cups,	o	6	8
Item, 6 Flafkits and 1 Maund k,	o	3	4
Item, 1 doz. Earthen Potts,	o	o	6
Item, 2 Staff Torches,	o	4	o
Item, for Yearbes l, 5 days,	o	1	8
Item, for Waferans, 5 days m,	o	1	8
Item, for Onions,	o	1	o

h Talwood and Bavings]. Chord-wood, and Bavins. See Dr. Birch's Life of Prince Henry: Wetwood and Bevins occur below, p. 184.

i Grains]. qu.

k Maund]. a large Bafket, now ufed for Apples, &c.

l Yearbes]. yerbs are often pronounced fo now; whence *Tirby Greafe*, for Herb of Grace.

m 5 days]. qu. perhaps gathering, or fetching them.

B b

Item,

	£.	s.	d.
Item, 2 Gallipots,	0	0	8
Item, for Yeaſt, 5 days,	0	1	8
Item, 20 doz. borrowed Veſſels,	0	5	1
Item, for Carriage of Wheat, Malt, Wine, and Wood, from the Water-ſide,	0	15	0
Item, for Parker the Cook, and other Cooks and Water-bearers,	4	10	0
Item, 6 doz. of Trenchers,	0	0	4
Firſt, for making a Cupboard,	0	1	4

ª Waferans]. v. above, p. 157.

The

The Charge of the said Sir John Nevile of Chete at
Lammas Aſſizes, in the 20th Year of the Reign of
King Henry the VIIIth.

	£.	s.	d.
Imprimis, in Wheat, 9 quarters,	12	0	0
Item, in Malt, 12 quarters,	10	0	0
Item, 5 Oxen,	6	13	4
Item, 24 Weathers,	3	4	0
Item, 6 Calves,		20	0
Item, 60 Capons of Greaſe,		25	0
Item, other Capons,	3	14	0
Item, 24 Pigs,	0	14	0
Item, 3 hogſheads of Wine,	8	11	8
Item, 22 Swans,	5	10	0
Item, 12 Cranes,	4	0	0
Item, 30 Heronſews,		30	0
Item, 12 Shovelards,		12	0
Item, 10 Bitters,		13	4
Item, 80 Partridges,		26	8
Item, 12 Pheaſants,		20	0
Item, 20 Curlews,		26	8
Item, Curlew Knaves 32,		32	0
Item, 6 doz. Plovers,	0	12	0
Item, 30 doz. Pidgeons,	0	7	6
Item, Mallards, Teal, and other Wild Fowl,		42	0
Item, 2 Baſkets of all manner of Spice,	5	0	0

B b 2   Item,

	£.	s.	d.
Item, in Malmſey, 24 Gallons,		32	0
Item, in Bucks,	10	0	0
Item, in Stags,	—	—	—

Fryday and Saturday.

	£.	s.	d.
Firſt, 3 couple of great Ling,		12	0
Item, 40 couple of Heberdine,		40	0
Item, Salt Sammon,		20	0
Item, Freſh Sammon and Great,	3	6	8
Item, 6 great Pike,		12	0
Item, 80 Pickerings,	4	0	0
Item, 300 great Breams,	15	0	0
Item, 40 Tenches,		26	8
Item, 80 Touling Eels and Brevet Eels, and 15 Ruds,		32	0
Item, a Firkin of Sturgeon,		16	0
Item, in Freſh Seals,		13	4
Item, 8 ſeame of Freſh Fiſh,	4	0	0
Item, 2 Bretts,		8	0
Item, a barrell of Green Ginger and Sucketts,		4	0
Item, 14 gallon of Vinegar,		7	7½
Item, 6 horſe-loads of Charcoal,		2	4
Item, 40 load of Wetwood and Bevins,		53	4
Item, for Salt,		5	2
Item, 6 doz. of Manchetts,		6	0
Item, Gingerbread for March Payne,		0	8
Item, 5 gallon of Muſtard,		2	6

Item,

	£.	s.	d.
Item, for loan of 6 doz. veffels,		5	2
Item, 3 gallons of Honey,		3	9
Item, for the cofts of Cooks and Water-bearers,	4	0	0
Item, for the Judges and Clerks of the Affize, for their Horfe-meat in the Inn, and for their Houfekeeper's meat, and the Clerk of the Affize Fee,	10	0	0
Item, for my Livery Coats, embroidered,	50	0	0
Item, for my Horfes Provender, Hay, Litter, and Grafs, at both the Affizes,	6	13	4

In

In a vellum MS. Account-Book of the Gild of the
Holy Trinity at Luton, com. Bedford, from
19 Hen. VIII. to the beginning of Ed. VI. there
are the expences of their Anniverfary Feafts, from
year to year, exhibiting the feveral Provifions,
with their prices. The feaft of 19 Hen. VIII. is
hereunder inferted; from whence fome judgement
may be formed of the reft.

	£.	s.	d.
5 quarters, 6 bufhels of Wheat,		50	2
3 bufhels Wheat Flower,	0	5	11
6 quarters malte,		29	0
72 Barrels Beer,	0	12	10
Brewing 6 quarters Malte,	0	4	0
Bakyng,	0	1	6
82 Geys,	1	0	7
47 Pyggs,	1	3	10
64 Capons,	1	9	8¼
74 Chekyns,	0	8	2
84 Rabetts, and Carriage,	0	10	8
Beyf,			
4 quarters,	1	0	0
a Lyfte,	0	0	8
a Shodour & Cromys,	0	0	11

Moton

	£.	s.	d.
Moton & Welle ª.			
1 quarter,	0	0	8
2 leggs of Welle & 2 Shodours,	0	1	0
A Marebone & Suet, & 3 Calwisfere,	0	0	4
1 quarter of Moton, and 6 Calwisfere,	0	0	9
20 Lamys,	1	5	10
Dreſſyng of Lamys,	0	0	6
Wine, 2 galons, a potell, & a pynte,	0	1	9
Wenegar 3 potellis,	0	1	0
Warg ᵇ 1 galon,	0	0	2½
Spyce,			
3 lb Pepur & half,	0	6	11
4 oz. of Clovis & Mace, & quartron,	0	3	4
11 lb. of Sugur & half,	0	7	0
½ lb. of Sinamon,	0	3	4
12 lb. of gret Refons,	0	1	0
6 lb. of fmale Refons,	0	1	4
½ lb. of Gynger,	0	1	10
½ lb. of Sandurs,	0	0	8
1 lb. of Lycoras,	0	0	6
4 lb. of Prunys,	0	0	8
1 lb. of Comfetts,	0	0	8
½ lb. of Turnefell,	0	0	8
1 lb. of Grenys,	0	1	9
1 lb. of Aneffeds,	0	0	5

ª Veal, now in the South pronounced with *W.*
ᵇ Verjuice.

2 lb.

	£.	s.	d.
2 lb. of Almonds,	0	0	5
2 oz. of Safron and a quartron,	0	2	9
2 lb. of Dats,	0	0	8
Eggs 600,	0	6	0
Butter,	0	2	7
Mylke 19 galons,	0	1	7
8 galons and 2 gal. of Crem,	0	1	3½
Hone 2 galons,	0	3	0
Salte ½ boſhell,	0	0	8
Fyſhe,			
Freſche, and the careeg from London,	0	3	8
A freſche Samon,	0	2	8
Salte Fyche for the Coks,	0	1	0
Rydyng for Trouts	0	0	8
Mynſtrels,	0	16	0
Butlers,	0	1	6
Cokys,	0	17	4

F I N I S.

For EU product safety concerns, contact us at Calle de José Abascal, 56–1°, 28003 Madrid, Spain or eugpsr@cambridge.org.

www.ingramcontent.com/pod-product-compliance
Ingram Content Group UK Ltd.
Pitfield, Milton Keynes, MK11 3LW, UK
UKHW010337140625
459647UK00010B/664